MW01438496

MOMENTS IN TIME

Copyright © 2014 by Neil Anthes
First Edition — May 2014

ISBN
978-1-4602-3920-9 (Hardcover)
978-1-4602-3921-6 (Paperback)
978-1-4602-3922-3 (eBook)

All rights reserved.

No part of this publication may be reproduced in any form, or by any means, electronic or mechanical, including photocopying, recording, or any information browsing, storage, or retrieval system, without permission in writing from the publisher.

Produced by:

FriesenPress
Suite 300 – 852 Fort Street
Victoria, BC, Canada V8W 1H8

www.friesenpress.com

Distributed to the trade by The Ingram Book Company

TABLE OF CONTENTS

Introduction i
Prologue iii

Part I
Peak Spiritual Experiences 1
    The Experiences 2
    Spiritually Transformative Experiences 8
    The Changes 13
    The Challenges 24
    More Adventures 35
    A String of Coincidences 38
    Summary 45

Part II
Daily Attitudes 47
    God's Will 48
    The Rules of the Game 52
    Infancy in Adulthood 54
    Fear 57
    A Swiss Bank Account 60
    Look and You Will See 63
    Embrace Your Disappointments 65
    Bad Habits 69
    Creating Gifts 73

Part III
Universal Energy 77
    A Subtle Impulse 78
    Creativity 82

TABLE OF CONTENTS CONTINUED...

Mirror Mirror 86
Natural Healing 89
Abundance and Expansion 91
More Abundance 93
The Food Buffet 97
It's Not Always About Me 101

Part IV
Inner Vision 107
    That Quiet Place 108
    Going to the Movies (A Love Story) 110
    The Holiday 113
    Forgiveness 116
    Scepticism 119
    Deception 122
    Accidents 125
    Body Memories 131
    Where Do All the Souls Come From? 134
    Ego and Soul 138
    Joy and Bliss 142

Epilogue 145
Conclusion 149

References 152

*Special thanks to the Shiraz Literary Society
for their help and encouragement with this book
particularly Mary, Michael and Johnie*

MOMENTS IN TIME

Reflections on Personal Mystical Experiences

NEIL ANTHES

*Brenda
Best wishes &
Happy Reading
Neil
10/24/14*

Introduction

*He who knows others is wise,
he who knows himself is enlightened.*

Lao Tzu

I was a university student in the late 1960s and early 1970s. It was a time of great social change and scientific achievement. Civil rights, the Vietnam War, recreational drug use, and space exploration were constant themes in the newspaper headlines. They were very interesting and challenging times. Social values and attitudes were shifting. Status quo was being questioned. As students, we often asked the question "Who are we?" After our studies were completed and we graduated, would we become engineers, computer programmers, scientists, teachers, optometrists, psychologists, urban planners, sociologists, or whatever it was we studied? Would we somehow become like a caterpillar, after years of study, and morph into a butterfly of our chosen field of endeavour?

Some of us did. We identified very deeply with the graduating degree that bore our name. Some of us did not make a strong emotional connection with our studies; we continued on in our quest to answer that question.

The opening line of the song Woodstock, written by Joni Mitchell in 1969 after the famed rock 'n' roll weekend in New

York State, reflected this question. The line is "I came upon a child of God."

Who are we really? Are we American, British, Canadian, Chinese, Russian, Vietnamese, Japanese, Australian, European, Italian, or African? Are we male or female? Are we the sons and daughters of Mr. and Mrs. George Smith or Geoffrey Jones? Are we Catholic, Protestant, Jewish, Buddhist, Hindu, or agnostic? Are we welders, car salesmen, teachers, ministers, nurses, doctors, soldiers, entertainers, columnists, carpenters, or news reporters?

We are all of these and none of these—at the same time. Yes, we become our professions, families and cultures, but we are also children of Creation, Divine Intelligence, The Universe, Grace, Universal Consciousness, or whatever you wish to call God. We live in two worlds simultaneously: the world of our physical senses, body, and cultures and the world of our spirit, soul, and Universal Consciousness.

This book describes my personal spiritual and mystical experiences with this Divine Universal Energy. These episodes started when I was a teenager and sporadically continued until my mid 50s. I continue to experience this energy daily to varying degrees. In Part I, I describe these happenings that are impossible to properly put into words and my responses or reactions to them. The remainder of the book is a collection of essays on spiritual philosophy and interpretations of my perceptions of our reality as a result of my experiences, personal meditation, contemplation, and reflection.

My hope is that by reading this book, you will gain a better understanding of yourself as a human being and that your relationship to the Divine will be made clearer. I also hope your mind will be expanded and the perception of your life will be changed for the better.

If you have had mystical experiences yourself, this book will help shed some light on your own situations. You will gain some comfort in knowing others have had similar experiences. Thus, it might help validate your episodes.

Prologue

I started writing this book two and a half years after my seventh experience with mystical cosmic consciousness. These episodes are described in the chapter entitled The Experiences. After that incident, I became addicted to reading. I wanted to find out what caused these blissful, indescribable feelings that I had been experiencing on and off for the past 40 years. I read books by such authors as—but not limited to—Dr Wayne Dyer, Eckhart Tolle, Deepak Chopra, Robin Sharma, Gary Zukov, Bruce Lipton, Gregg Braden, Caroline Myss, James Allen, and many other writers on mysticism whose books I had bought years earlier but never read.

As a result of these readings and other books I have read over the preceding years, I became aware that many other people have had similar experiences with this mysterious and divine energy. We do not seem to hear from these people very often. I decided it was important to record what I have been experiencing as an example and hopefully provide some validation for others. These experiences are indeed divine in nature and not devilish in any way shape or form, although they can be very overwhelming and perplexing at the time.

This cosmic energy has been well researched for many years, yet it does not get reported or embraced by contemporary academic communities or by contemporary religious thought. Reading the chapters in this book and reflecting upon some of your own life experiences, you'll come to understand that there is divine guidance available to all humanity, individually and collectively. This guidance is beyond the physical senses, but we can very much perceive it with our inner eye on a day-to-day basis.

While reading Wayne Dyer's book, Wisdom of the Ages, I read a quote from Cicero. For those of you who don't know who Cicero was, he lived from 106 BC – 43 BC. Wayne Dyer describes him as "a Roman statesman and man of letters; he was considered Rome's greatest orator and its most articulate philosopher. The last years of the republican Rome are often referred to as the Age of Cicero." The quote follows:

The Six Mistakes of Man

1. The illusion that personal gain is made up of crushing others.

2. The tendency to worry about things that cannot be changed or corrected.

3. Insisting that a thing is impossible because we cannot accomplish it.

4. Refusing to set aside trivial preferences.

5. Neglecting development and refinement of the mind, and not acquiring a habit of reading and study.

6. Attempting to compel others to believe and live as we do.[1]

After reading this quote, I realized that everything he said still applies today. I put the book down and I felt very, very old as a human being. It seems we have learned very little in the past 2000 years.

This passage motivated me to start writing this book, although I had no idea where it would go. I wanted to at least put my experiences in writing and offer them to anyone who felt a need to hear about them. There was also another reason I wrote this book. On a regular basis, I would get a message as I was meditating. That message was always the same. It would say

"Write a Book!"
I hope you find this enjoyable and enlightening.

PART I
PEAK SPIRITUAL EXPERIENCES

The Experiences

I had just walked by two small gravestone markers, hugging the ground, on the edge of the narrow trail that led to an open grassy meadow. The forest was slowly reclaiming its space as the roots of the trees were growing over them like wooden fingers grasping the chiselled stone. Just as I reached the meadow, I perceived in my consciousness an extremely long thin arm, radiating brilliant white light, reaching towards me. A hand appeared and then a finger emerged which gently touched me on the top of my head, an electrifying transformative touch. I was immediately immersed in a feeling of rapture, joy, unconditional love, and bliss—nothing like I had felt before. I suddenly seemed to be under a very large and powerful microscope, on a flat glass slide, laying on my back peering up through hundreds of times magnification directly into the eye of God. The eye was both soft and gazing, not defined on the edges, and filled the frame of my observation. The colour purple diffused around a large translucent black pupil, which appeared to be a window looking out over another vast expansive universe, something that included me. I felt extremely small, like a speck of dust, but at the same time very large, part of something greater. It seemed like the eye of God and I were separated by a distance of millions and millions of miles, yet we were together in this grassy meadow. Two contradictory sensations of small and infinitely large took over my perception and being. The entire experience is impossible to describe, yet it has remained with me all my life. To seemingly travel to the edge of the universe and back in a few moments seemed surreal; it was what I perceived as

MOMENTS IN TIME | 3

an out-of-body experience. To experience such an episode was beyond anything that my imagination could have pondered. As quickly as it had started, it vanished, and I was again a prisoner of my five senses, but in awe of my mysterious but magnificent moment.

At the time, I was 17 years old on a camping trip with my family in the Maritime Provinces of Canada. It was a warm, late June evening at about 7:30. The forest was at the edge of a campground on the north shore of the Bay of Fundy, New Brunswick.

I questioned what had happened. What had I just experienced? Neither school, church, family, nor friends had ever mentioned anything like this!

I was the third child of six in a typical 1950s - 1960s North American family. Children were expected to adopt the values of their parents without question. They had never mentioned anything similar to my experience! I was taught that God was in Heaven. My teenage perception was if you got past Judgement Day, you would sit with Him in Heaven. Yet I just met God in a field in New Brunswick!

I was now in a dilemma. My father, an elder in the church, demanded that we attend church every Sunday. However, the dogma of the church did not appeal to me at the best of times, and now after my episode by the Bay of Fundy, its appeal was even less. The arguments with my father about going to church grew more intense. As long as I was living at home, Sunday mornings at church was a waste of my time. My challenge was to learn about what I had experienced.

A new journey had begun, even though at the time I was unaware of it.

Seven years later, my journey led me to Eastern philosophy and the practice of meditation. While reading a book by Gopi Krishna about his experiences after meditating for many years, I came across this quote:

"... Suddenly, with a roar like that of a waterfall, I felt a stream of liquid light entering my brain through the spinal cord. Entirely unprepared for such a development, I was completely taken by surprise; by regaining self-control instantaneously,

I remained sitting in the same posture, keeping my mind on the point of concentration. The illumination grew brighter and brighter, the roaring louder ... I felt the point of consciousness that was myself growing wider, surrounded by waves of light. It grew wider and wider, spreading outward while the body, normally the immediate object of its perception, appeared to have receded into the distance until I became entirely unconscious of it ... I was no longer myself, or to be more accurate, no longer as I knew myself to be, a small point of light in the state of awareness confined in the body, but instead was a vast circle of consciousness in which the body was but a point, bathed in light and in a state of exaltation and happiness impossible to describe." [2]

In this passage, he was describing a Kundalini experience, something I had never heard about before. This really grabbed my attention and my imagination. In his writings, Gopi Krishna points out that having a direct experience with Kundalini energy is rare. It is not a guaranteed result of meditation. Many people meditate all their lives and do not have such a mystical occurrence. Despite the odds, I decided to try and have such an experience in my life. I dedicated myself to meditating three times a day wherever I was. At the time, I was employed as a pharmaceutical sales representative and spent many hours driving between doctors' offices. During these times, I would imagine and fantasize with excitement the possibility of experiencing the "state of exaltation and happiness impossible to describe" that Gopi Krishna had written about.

In the late spring, shortly after my 29th birthday, I awoke at 4 o'clock in the morning. This was very unusual, as I was a very sound sleeper. My body was in a state of sexual arousal. As I was about to shift my body, the base of my spine started tingling. The sensation grew more and more intense until suddenly, even though my eyes were closed, I perceived a flash of yellowy-silver light that surrounded my entire being. At the same time, a roar in my ears started. It sounded like the combined resonance of the buzz of a huge hive of bees and the flow of a massive waterfall like Niagara Falls. My heart raced with excited anticipation. Was I in the starting mode of a real Kundalini experience?

The light grew brighter, and the sound increased in volume. The noise became so loud that for a moment I felt fearful. The entire experience stopped abruptly, like someone had turned off an electrical light switch. My lower spine ached and continued to ache for several days. The real ache was in my heart. My dream of experiencing the state of "exaltation and happiness impossible to describe" had been shattered by my fear.

Getting over my disappointment with myself, I decided that if the experience should start to happen again, I would try to control my fear. I continued to meditate and again started to imagine having a Kundalini experience. My mid-afternoon meditation was always a challenge. I often meditated in my car in parking lots and public parks. I even meditated at shopping malls. If someone saw me, it would look like I was taking an afternoon nap! One of the institutions I called on as a sales representative at the time was a psychiatric hospital. I even meditated in the washroom of that hospital from time to time!

By the grace of spirit, several weeks later, I again awoke at 4 o'clock in the morning. My body was in the same state. The tingling at the base of the spine began, the lights in my perception exploded, and the roaring in my ears began and got louder and louder and louder. Again, my fear erupted and the light switch went off. Again my disappointment with myself was crushing. I had lost my second chance to my fear. I assumed I was not destined to have such an experience, despite my intense desire for such an episode.

The Universe, however, had another plan. A few weeks later, I awoke again at 4 o'clock. My body was in a state of sexual arousal, my lower spine was tingling, the lights were exploding, and the roaring had begun. This time when my fear arrived, I did not acknowledge it; I would not allow it to enter into my consciousness. I focused on the sensations that were developing within myself. I shifted my body and rested on my back and listened and observed the transformation that was going on in my field of perception. Yellowy-silver light swirled and danced in front of my closed eyes. The roaring became very loud but pleasant, and a feeling of indescribable joy enveloped my being. After what seemed like only a minute or two, the roaring subsided. The lights were dimmed. My spine stopped tingling. I returned to my sleep, grateful and humbled by the experience that Gopi Krishna described as a "state of exaltation and happiness impossible to describe."

Two years later, I had the opportunity meet with Gopi Krishna privately in Toronto. I described my experiences and asked his advice. His response was brief: he said I was at that age when the energy is quick. He then leaned back into his chair, looked me in the eye, and just smiled!

At that age. Yes, I had read in books that the energy was most active around the age of 30. Dr. Maurice Burke in his book, Cosmic Consciousness, presents his research and found that 90 percent of people in history who showed signs of enlightenment did so around that age.[3] I had no further experiences and concluded my time had passed. I was very thankful for what I had experienced.

My meditations became less frequent, although not totally abandoned. My focus began to shift away from the inner world to the outer world of career and materialism. The years started to drift by.

Twenty-five years had now passed since my experience by the Bay of Fundy. During that twenty-fifth year, something shifted in my consciousness. I had recently joined the Toastmasters club that my wife had joined a few years earlier. One of the members was a lady who was my age. Coincidentally, we were both born in the same hospital. As a result of this, I had always felt a kinship with her. While talking with this friend after a Toastmasters meeting in the late spring, I was caught completely by surprise. My spirit suddenly expanded like a huge cosmic rubber band to the very top of the highest mountain in creation. I was both in my body carrying on a conversation and a million miles away simultaneously. My inner perception saw the mountain top as warm and rocky, and there was an abundant array of yellow and orange wildflowers at my feet. Everything was surrounded by a soft light that reminded me of deep dusk on a summer's evening in the extreme northern latitudes. Like that transitioning magenta and purple light that remains all through the night. The light bathed all the lower surrounding mountain ranges as they stretched out into infinity. Whether I was on earth or another planet, I couldn't tell. I was at a very expansive place where I could perceive the cosmic horizon. One year later, while talking with the same friend, again my soul expanded. This time, it visited the depths of the deepest ocean trench in the Pacific Ocean in the blink of an eye. I was again in two places simultaneously, at a great distance apart. I could perceive the height of the underwater mountains as very long dark shadows on either side of the canyon. Shadows reaching up like huge hands towards the surface, with peaks as pointed fingers piercing through the waters. The water was not black but appeared as a clear deep blue colour and permeated my entire perception. It was sprinkled with speaks of bright silver, not unlike a gently falling snow, but frozen in space, not moving. I was again overwhelmed with the perception of infinite expansiveness. During each of these episodes, I was showered with the feelings of joy, bliss, and unconditional love. For several months after this episode, whenever I met this woman, I would for a very brief moment perceive her soul, her spirit, her grace, and her essence and feel that deep Divine Joy.

During these two incidences with my friend when I was embraced by the bliss of Grace, my feelings were exactly the same as I had felt at the Bay of Fundy twenty five years earlier when I was 17 years old.

Four months later, while visiting a friend who had worked as an assistant to Gopi Krishna, I had another Kundalini experience in the early morning hours. This time, there was no roaring sound in my ears—only brilliant, dancing silvery yellow light in my visual perception and a tingling sensation all along my spine, as well as that wonderful "state of exaltation and happiness impossible to describe."

An older abandoned journey was reawakened!

Spiritually Transformative Experiences

There is an organization in Alpine California called the American Center for the Integration of Spiritually Transformative Experiences (ACISTE). Their website references a 2004 survey by the National Opinion Research Center at the University of Chicago that discovered 35.7 percent of the adult US population has had at least one religious or spiritual experience "that changed their life." [4] In another survey done five years later, in 2009, by the Pew Forum on Religion and Public Life, they found almost half of all participants claimed to have had a mystical or spiritual experience, more than double in the last fifty years. [5] There appears to be an increasing awareness of our spiritual connections or people are at least feeling more comfortable admitting socially to an experience that is very personal and perplexing.

The ACISTE group refers to these experiences as Spiritually Transformative Experiences. They define a Spiritually Transformative Experience or STE as "An experience is spiritually transformative when it causes people to perceive themselves and the world profoundly differently; by expanding the individual's identity, augmenting their sensitivities, and thereby altering their values, priorities and appreciation of the purpose of life. This may be triggered by surviving clinical death, or by otherwise sensing an enlarged reality. There are many types and many names for experiences that can share common features and can be catalysts for spiritual transformation, near-death experiences [NDE's] near-death like experiences [NDLDs] out of body experiences [OBEs], visions, spiritual emergencies, awakenings, Kundalini experiences ... past life experiences ... after death communication ... etc."[6]

When I read these words on the website, I concluded that my episodes were most definitely spiritually transformative! The ACISTE website identifies many of the changes following a STE and the many challenges that accompany such experiences.

The changes are generally not sudden, but may evolve over many years of integrating and reflecting upon the meaning, messages, and values derived from the experience. Some of the changes that may occur according to the information posted are:

> ***Strengthened spiritual or religious values***
> ***Improved behaviour and attitude towards others***
> ***Changes in values***
> ***A greater sense of well-being***
> ***A more positive outlook on life***
> ***A greater desire to learn***
> ***Increased creativity***
> ***Increased psychic awareness*** [7]

The website goes on to describe some of the common challenges that occur following an STE. I have used their descriptions for those conditions, as follows:[8]

Common Challenges Following an STE

As part of the integration process that leads to positive changes and transformation following a spiritually transformative experience, an experiencer may also have to deal with one or more challenges. The intensity, scope, or absence of the challenges depends on many factors including the age or health of the experiencer, their cultural background beliefs and attitudes prior to the experience, the content of the experience, and/or how the experience was accepted by one's significant relationships including spouses, parents, friends, colleagues, doctors, clergy, or therapists. The following is a list and description of possible challenges faced by people who had one or more spiritually transformative experiences.

Common challenges include:

Possessing a radical shift in reality
Issues related to sharing the experience
Changes in religious views
Changes in attitudes towards healing
Increased sensitivity to electricity, chemicals, smells etc.
Problems dealing with psychic abilities

Expanding on these challenges is the following:

Possessing a radical shift in reality

A spiritually transformative experience can be a dramatic and complete immersion into a reality unlike anything experienced in one's life previously. As a result of this experience, experiencers may undergo a permanent and complete paradigm shift in their views of their roles in life, reality, and what happens when they die.

Issues related to sharing the experience

One of the most common challenges experiencers face are those related to labelling, describing, and sharing their experiences. Most experiencers deal with invalidating, uninformed, or otherwise harm-producing responses or do not share them at all for fear of invalidation. The need to disclose or share the experience, especially immediately afterwards, may be intense, especially with one's loved ones. Their response can greatly influence whether or when the experiencer chooses to share his or her experience again.

Changes in religious views

Experiencers may no longer hold conventional views of "heaven," "hell," "God," "evil," or "sin." In one study, 78 percent of near-death experiencers said their attitudes about their religious upbringing changed following their NDEs.

Changes in attitudes towards healing

While little research has been done in this area, some experiencers change their attitudes in what causes or heals disease. Many experiencers become healers using energy, visualization, intuitive, or other alternative approaches to standard medical treatments.

Increased sensitivity to electricity, chemicals, smells, etc.

Many experiencers report a heightened sensitivity to electricity, chemicals, smells, loud noises, etc. They frequently describe difficulties readjusting into previously "normal" environments, job settings, situations, and events. Some report new allergies or sensitivities to chemicals and smells. Many turn to organic foods and avoid perfume and scented or chemically treated products.

Problems dealing with psychic abilities

Many experiencers reported the emergence of psychic abilities after their STE. The abilities may include:

> *Intuitive, auditory, or visual knowledge of what is or what is to come*
> *Mediumship*
> *Telepathy*
> *Seeing auras*
> *Ability to communicate with animals*

Automatic writing

While many people may embrace or seek these abilities, that is not necessarily the case with some experiencers. These abilities can surprise and disrupt one's customary thought processes and actions. Some may adjust them into their lives or turn them into careers, accepting them as gifts, while others describe how they prayed to be "left alone."

I discovered this material at the ACISTE website in 2012. When I reflect on these points, I know I have experienced many issues, qualities, and challenges mentioned that I will share in the following chapters.

The Changes

When I look at the list of changes and challenges compiled by the American Center for the Integration of Spiritually Transformative Experiences, I see some of myself in all of those qualities. Some qualities were immediate; others evolved with time and after more experiences. My belief in a spiritual realm is unwavering as a result of my episodes. This belief is developing and evolving into a greater sense of well-being and a greater sense of purpose. I have tried to improve my attitude towards others and develop greater compassion, as these are certainly qualities I strive to attain. Creativity in the form of writing, photography, and painting now plays a major role in my life. I have studied photography worldwide with many different professional photographers and taken up painting with acrylics.

When I examine this list of qualities, two strike me as being particularly relevant to my experience: increased psychic awareness and a greater desire to learn.

Increased Psychic Awareness

After my experience on the shores of the Bay of Fundy, one of the first things to emerge was my psychic abilities. I began to have premonitions, such as hearing bits and pieces of conversations days or weeks before they happened. I would glimpse small portions of activities prior to the event. I would also perceive faces of influential people and girlfriends I would meet 3 to 6 months later. I would experience these events as I was going off to sleep at night.

Déjà vu, that "been here before" feeling, became part of my life. I would often arrive at a city or town for the first time and it would feel very familiar. When my family and I were in Bathurst, New Brunswick during that trip to the Maritimes, we crossed a long bridge. As we began to cross, I knew there was a left turn off of this bridge to an island in the river, even though we had never been there before. I would attend an event or social gathering and have a sense that I had experienced this before.

I seemed to have become sensitive in other ways. The phone would ring and I would know who was there before they spoke. This was before call display! I would walk into a room and know immediately if somebody was angry. I would drive through a strange city and drive blind, turning right or left on a whim, and arrive at my destination. No GPS then! All of these experiences were very baffling, appeared so illogical, and were beyond any type of real explanation. I started to call these phenomenons the "Ooky Spookies."

The Ooky Spookies developed even more when I started to meditate three times a day. I became very sensitive to what I would call "spiritual direction," an intuition which continues to this day. By spiritual direction, I mean having a gut feel, a hunch, or an intuitive thought or feeling about something that appears very illogical at the time. For example, when I was a sales representative for a pharmaceutical company, one morning just after I awoke, I had a gut feeling to travel to a city that defied logic. The doctors in that city did not attend their offices on a Wednesday. This was a Wednesday morning. Nevertheless, I decided to follow my intuition. When I arrived in the city, I remembered a physician that I was having trouble seeing. He was never in his office when I called. I decided to stop by his office to see if he was there and sure enough he was, and he took my call. I was required to do a minimum number of calls each day, and logically, spending a Wednesday in that city would not allow that to happen. Somehow, I completed my day with more than the minimum calls required. This was something that completely defied all reason.

When I travel, I often find food products I enjoy. When I get home, I try to find them, but they are often not available locally. I recently spent some time in the southwestern area of the United States and enjoyed a fairly healthy (for junk food) snack. Upon returning home, I started looking for it; however, it was nowhere to be found. On these quests after returning home, I usually try about five different stores before I give up. I was on my last trip attempting to find this snack product. I was sitting at a stop sign waiting to turn left when I had a gut feel to turn right. I did. A mile down the road was a small grocery store. I stopped and went in. They had what I was looking for!

In my mid-20s, I needed a job. I held a real estate license, but the market was extremely slow so I decided to apply for a salaried position at my local real estate board. I was walking down the street towards the office when I passed a store selling pianos. I played piano since I was four and had a feeling that I should go into the store. I walked in and enquired about employment. As it turned out, the owner had just found out that an employee at another of his stores was leaving. He hired me on the spot.

In 2004, I had knee surgery. The joint was infected during surgery, which led to another emergency surgery. It took many months and eventually years before my knee returned to some sense of normal. During my rehabilitation, I would go to my local gym religiously every day for an hour. One morning, I had a gut feel not to go, so I didn't. Shortly after, someone called enquiring about some photographic equipment I had for sale—and bought it!

When my wife was managing her medical diagnostics business, she would often travel overseas for a week at a time. During one of her trips, I was driving to work in the morning and I had an intuitive feeling to turn around and go to my wife's office. At that time her business partner was very ill with a brain tumour. He was hospitalized and completely incapacitated. He could no longer read or write or contribute to the business. I turned my car around and drove to her office. When I arrived, the office manager was very distraught. She asked me into her office. She closed the door and almost broke into tears. It was payday. She had forgotten to ask my wife to sign the checks. The other signing partner was incapable. Fortunately due to her partner's illness, just before my wife left for her trip, I had been added as a signing authority to the bank account. I signed the cheques! As you can imagine, the office manager was extremely relieved.

    My wife and I are avid photographers, especially when we travel. During a visit to Cape Town South Africa, we wanted to photograph the unique colourful change huts found on the beaches in the area. My wife likes to be very thoughtful in composing her images; I like to work more quickly. At this particular location, it seemed we were getting into each other's way. I decided to walk to a bridge that overlooked the beach about a quarter of a mile away. As is often the case with photography, some potential subjects caught my eye as I walked to the bridge. After about 15 minutes, I arrived. I was photographing in the opposite direction of the beach when I had a strong intuitive feeling to go and look at the beach. It took a minute, but I spotted my wife among the change huts. She was walking slowly, putting down her tripod, lining up a shot, and then moving 10 feet to her left doing the same thing. She then walked about 30 feet to her right, put her tripod down and composed a shot. She was photographing in front of the huts. There was a person at the back of the huts, which seemed normal as this was a public beach. However, I soon noticed he was moving in exactly the same sequence as my wife! He was stalking her, but out of her sight! I immediately started running as fast as I could toward her. The stranger must have seen me because when I got to where my wife was, he was gone!

    Do I always follow my intuitive hunches and gut feelings? I wish I could say yes. Sometimes they seem far-fetched, require more effort than I want to put in at the time, appear highly illogical, or I'm just too far into a situation to change. For example, I was employed by a British manufacturer of anaesthetic equipment to oversee their Canadian operations and later the United States operations. Our products were sold and distributed through a network of dealers across North America. We received an unsolicited offer of interest from a Canadian company to represent our product line across Canada. As with any dealer network, you have strong locations and weaker locations. Our sales were flat in Canada, so the head office asked me to pursue this letter of interest. We held discussions over several weeks that led to a distribution proposal that was eventually accepted by both sides.

I must admit, I let the cat out of the bag by phoning the most successful dealer from our current network to discuss my company's plans for the future. I wanted to thank him for his support over the years, but we had to look at the entire national operation. This led to some hastily requested meetings by our current dealer network, to which we obliged. The meeting was held at head office in England, with the current dealer network President attending. He presented his case as to why we should not change but continue with his national network. The managing director of my company promised them an immediate decision.

The management team that I was a member of huddled in another room to discuss the situation. It was now decision time. As manager of the territory, I was asked the final question: should we make the change? My gut intuitive feeling surprised me. It said absolutely not! Stay with the current dealer network! That was not what I was expecting. However, after months of negotiation and travelling between two continents, I could not come up with any logical reasons as to why we should not proceed. I had pushed for the dealer change. We all had put many hours into the project. I flew thousands of miles in cramped airplanes. That afternoon I ignored my intuition. I recommended we go ahead with our decision for change. After all, we had worked very hard on this for many months. We had considered the options and ramifications of staying put or heading down a different path. All the possibilities had been examined in detail. It was the right direction for the company, so I thought.

Our new dealer network became a reality. They were trained, given support material, and we looked forward to many successes in the marketplace. Almost immediately, the people with whom we had been negotiating who had always returned our phone calls within minutes were now taking days to respond. Communications from the new network seemed to be nonexistent. Sales started to slide. Sales representative turnover increased alarmingly. Sales continue to slide. Within a year, the Canadian operation was closed. I was unemployed! I should have followed my intuition that afternoon in England!

Not all intuitive feelings are as dramatic. Sometimes, they are just about day-to-day things. For example, I do the grocery shopping in our household. Sometimes, I have a feeling that pushes me to go to a different store than usual, and I'll find a product I was looking for or one I use at a better price. I have a middle and high-frequency hearing impairment, a result of too many very loud rock band concerts when I was younger. I wear hearing aids in certain situations. When leaving the house to attend a meeting one evening, I had a gut feeling to change the batteries, but I didn't. The batteries went dead halfway through the meeting.

Another example of not following my intuitive feelings happened when we were trying to sell our house in 2003. We lived in West Kelowna, British Columbia and had just purchased a new home in the nearby community of Peachland. We were not in a rush to sell, as we considered renting our house if we couldn't get our price. Shortly after it was put on the market, we received a call. A gentleman from Europe was interested in our property and wanted an appointment to discuss a possible sale. The agent didn't have an offer; the gentleman did not want to put one on the table. Although unusual, we made the appointment.

When they arrived, this European gentleman started telling us stories about houses he bought and sold in Germany. He rambled on and on for 45 minutes. I was getting rather impatient and wondered where all of this dialogue was going. His stories had one common theme: the asking price of properties he had purchased was basically ignored. When he finally got around to talking about our property, he put a verbal offer on the table, much lower than we would consider. He left. The next day, the agent called–the offer had been increased to above our minimum threshold, but still below what we wanted. I flatly rejected it. Even though my quiet inner intuitive voice was telling me to accept the offer, I ignored it! Our house bordered a forest, which was tinder dry. One month later, a huge forest fire hit our area. Over the next several weeks, the fire destroyed over 200 homes. We were very stressed out trying to keep a watch on two homes. Just after the fire passed through town and continued to burn up the mountainside, we received a call from someone who wanted to look at our house. After some negotiation, we accepted an offer that was 10 percent less than what the European gentleman had offered. If I had only followed my intuition, we would have been less stressed out during the fire and had more dollars in our pockets!

As interesting as these intuitive events are from my perspective, the most amazing aspect of the emerging psychic abilities that resulted from my spiritually transformative experiences started to occur when I committed myself to meditating. I seemed to be developing a rather unusual sensitivity to other people's thoughts. As I mentioned earlier, I was a pharmaceutical sales representative at the time, calling on pharmacists and physicians. I began to notice that I would sense a question before it was verbalized by the person I was talking with. When I finally realized this was happening, it certainly helped me to prepare my answer before the question was asked. One day, during a discussion with a physician, I sensed his forthcoming question. As we were talking, I found myself formulating my answer to the question and in the process my attention drifted away from him entirely. Then I proceeded to verbalize my answer to his query. His response was not the normal, happy expression of someone who just received a clarification of an issue—he looked like he had just seen a ghost! I suddenly realized he had not yet asked his question!

I never did that again!

From then on, I would introduce the answer to a sensed question as if it was a normal progression of our discussion or I would say that one of his colleagues asked me about this point and I thought he might be concerned as well. This sensitivity lessened when my mediation became less frequent.

Today I continually get hunches, gut feelings, and intuitive feelings about issues I am addressing, from simple daily activities to long term projects. When I follow them, sometimes it seems meaningless; sometimes I run into friends; or sometimes it helps me accomplish a goal I had or occasionally it leads me to help someone out. The challenge is always differentiating the real gut feel from an idle thought. This is not always easy. The intuitive feeling is often illogical. It is softer than an idle thought. It is less demanding and does not run into more ideas about the subject. It stays put after saying its piece. It does not trigger any more reasoning. The intuitive gut feeling always has a different quality that is difficult to describe. It is very subtle.

After my spiritually transformative experiences, all of these different psychic episodes and happenings that emerged were a dramatic change for me. Premonitions, the sense of déjà vu, increased sensitivities to others and especially intuitive hunches were all very mysterious and fascinating. It took some time for me to get used to this new reality that was occurring within me. It also took some time before I accepted this as part of my human nature. It was, upon reflection, an exciting personal change.

A Great Desire to Learn

The second major quality of spiritually transformative experiences to emerge for me was a great desire to learn. For me, that was to try to learn and understand what had happened at the Bay of Fundy and during my subsequent very expansive out-of-body experiences that created the same sensations as that first episode. The Kundalini experiences were something I pursued after learning about them. My out-of-body experiences were something I was unaware of before they happened. They were spontaneous events that happened on their own with no effort on my part. I wondered, "Were all these episodes somehow related?" I was driven to try and find answers to my questions.

Pre-university education was fairly easy for me; I was accelerated in grade school and generally excelled in mathematics and science. However, I started losing interest in math and sciences after my experience at 17. Yet I entered university as a physics and chemistry major. By the beginning of my second year, I had had enough of all the calculating involved with mathematics and sciences and switched to biology and psychology. Psychology fascinated me. By the time I was ready to graduate, I was one statistics course short of qualifying for a Bachelor of Arts degree in Psychology. However, I opted to take a Bachelor of Science degree as I thought it would create more opportunities in the real world.

It was four years after University that I was introduced to the ideas and practices of meditation, Eastern philosophy, Western astrology and the writings of Dr. Emmet Fox.

Meditation and contacting the spirit within were contrary to my religious upbringing that taught that the spirit (God) is outside of you. The concept of universal law helped explain some of the road blocks I had experienced in my life after graduating. I was putting little effort into various jobs and wondering why I was getting small results—as you sow, so shall you reap!

Western astrology for me was a personality theory that showed more insight into personality structure than anything I studied in university from Rogers, Freud, or Maslow.

The writings of Dr. Emmet Fox appealed to me. His interpretations of Biblical passages were very relevant for day to day living. Dr. Fox was an ordained Divine Science minister and author who preached in New York City starting in 1931. People would line up to hear his sermons. He spoke to crowds of up to four thousand people at a time at the Manhattan Opera House and Carnegie Hall. His sermons never lasted more than 20 minutes. His book, The Ten Commandments, shows very clearly how our consciousness determines our experiences in life. At that time in my life, his writings gave the scriptures new meaning. They became practical and alive. The Bible became a manual for daily inspiration and guidance, more than just the word of God as I had been told in church. I was learning a new way of interpreting my traditional religious upbringing.

I was given new tools to explore my life, with concepts such as a spiritual force within ourselves, universal law (we are responsible for our lives), and the framework for self-knowledge through the symbolism of Western astrology. The writing of Emmet Fox also added a new dimension. With my experiences of déjà vu, premonitions, and spiritual directions, the concept of a spiritual force within my own self was something I wanted to and started to explore.

I meditated and read books about psychic phenomenon, spiritual healing, Eastern philosophy, auras, chakras, mystical experiences, and Kirlian photography. I trained to do clairvoyant readings, therapeutic touch, and perceive auras. I learned self-hypnosis. In my attempt to see how others handled this energy, I visited mediums. Also, a local United Church held laying-on-of-hands services every Monday evening. I would attend those services and observe people being administered to by the healers. Nobody threw away their crutches and sprinted out the door. They just seemed to feel better and appear more peaceful after their sessions were completed. Somehow the energy flowed from healers to those seeking help and produced a sense of calm and well being. The drive to learn was very strong and continues to this day. It has led me to many new perceptions on life, some of which I will share in last three parts of this book.

One of the groups I joined during this time frame was the Association for Research and Enlightenment (ARE) founded by Edgar Cayce in 1931. Edgar Cayce lived from 1877 – 1945 and has been described as the "sleeping prophet," the father of holistic medicine. [9] For more than 40 years, Cayce gave psychic readings to thousands of people while in an unconscious state, diagnosing illnesses and revealing past lives and prophecies yet to come. If there is some sort of spiritual mystical energy residing within ourselves and responsible for psychic phenomenon and mystical experience, what is it? The Cayce readings provided insight into this.

The Cayce readings covered many subjects, the majority related to holistic health in the treatment of illness. Other main subject areas included philosophy and reincarnation, dreams and dream interpretation, ESP, psychic phenomenon and spiritual growth, and meditation and prayer. It seemed as if Cayce had an ability to tap into a vast sea of spiritual knowledge through a faculty of intuition, a faculty beyond the reasoning, logical mind. Many of Cayce's suggestions for healing, considered quackery at the time, have been validated by medical science today, such as using electrical current to heal broken bones. [10]

In a magazine published by the ARE in the early 1990s, it was suggested that upon death, we go through a review of our lives. We are asked some questions, two of which are "How have I learned to love?" and "What wisdom have I gained?" These questions stayed with me for many years, and after my experience with my Toastmaster friend, it occurred to me to ask these questions while alive rather than waiting until death. Dr. Brian Weiss in his book Many Lives, Many Masters, relates a quote from one of the Masters: "knowledge practised becomes wisdom." [11]

Perhaps the key to life is to practise!

In the book The Edgar Cayce Handbook by Mark Thurston and Christopher Fazel, the authors state "the Spirit is alive in the midst of daily living, if only we'll recognize it ... Individual growth and development may be realized through a harmonious interplay of personal effort on one hand and a surrender to a higher power on the other." [12]

By pursuing my desire to learn about my experiences, I have discovered that we constantly learn just by living everyday. I see a constant realigning of my perspective on life. I realize we collectively share not only our physical space but also a common spiritual creative source.

The Challenges

The biggest challenges for me after all of the episodes were: sharing the experiences, the changes in my religious and spiritual views, my attitude towards healing, my sensitivity to electricity, chemicals and smells, and my initial problems in dealing with my psychic abilities.

Sharing the Experiences

The biggest initial challenge after the Bay of Fundy experience as a teenager was trying to share the experience. I wanted to discover if others had had similar experiences, and to find an explanation. At that time in my life, my interests were very different from my family in general. I was raised on classical music, traditional religion and accepting the status quo–traditions were honoured. There is absolutely nothing wrong with this at all and I learned some very important values that I continue to honour today. Values such as respect and consideration for others, volunteering at your chosen church or organization and just being helpful as situations arise were part of my upbringing and have stayed with me throughout my life.

However, my music interests were rock 'n' roll. Although I did not dislike classical music, my preference was popular music. I also enjoyed watching sports from the time I was a small boy. I would watch football on television and be convinced that the players had to be in high school! I played little league baseball.

My father, however, had no interest in sports whatsoever and no interest in rock 'n' roll music. As a matter fact, I was often reminded that rock 'n' roll music was not appropriate for a Sunday. Any big sporting events usually found me at the house of my best friend, whose father was an avid sports fan. I seemed to have less in common with my family. I was also the only boy in the family for the first 14 years of my life. How was I, "the odd one," to share this mysterious and profound experience with my family–I didn't!

Two years after my Bay of Fundy episode, at the urging of my father, I attended a weekend retreat sponsored by the church. It was a regional function, so there were people from many different churches including our own. During the first evening, I mustered up the courage to share my experience with someone I thought to be a complete stranger. He was unknown to me, but as it turned out he was a work colleague of my father. This man expressed great relief that I had shared my experiences with him; however, he had a very grave look on his face. He informed me very emphatically that my experiences were the "work of the devil." He assured me that I could be saved and not to panic. The following week, he sent a book home with my father called the Challenging Counterfeit. The cat was out of the bag. My sisters saw the book, and questions were asked. I shared only my psychic abilities of premonitions, the sense of déjà vu and feelings that future events were going to happen; I did not relate my experience on the shores of the Bay of Fundy. I didn't read the book!

I have four sisters, two younger and two older. The older ones seemed somewhat subdued and made little or no comment. The younger ones seemed somewhat interested. My parents made no comments at all. Sometimes, no reaction is just as good as a positive reaction.

As for my perception on the "work of the devil," I knew this was not the case. The expansiveness, feelings of love, bliss, and wonderment of the whole experience cannot be the work of an evil force. They can only be the work of a loving, creative intelligence. This incident did not stop me from trying to find people who were experiencing similar phenomena. However, I shared only the psychic outcome of my experience, not the actual experience itself. Sometimes I would talk about and share my premonitions with people at work on a slow Friday afternoon. They would often be somewhat distant come Monday morning! I found few people willing to acknowledge such abilities may exist for mankind. Most considered the idea spooky, some feared it, some found it amusing, and others would just walk away.

My last attempt at trying to find answers within the traditional framework of knowledge (family, church, school, science) happened when I was hired as a pharmaceutical representative. I traveled to the head office for two weeks of training. The first evening before class started I had dinner with the head of the training department. He was well versed in our psychiatric drug line. He seemed intelligent and we shared a common interest in psychology. I started talking about my premonitions and how often there was a strong persistent feeling that something would transpire in the future. This event would be neither good nor bad, just an event. He made no comment, so the conversation was brief. The next day, he was teaching and presenting the symptoms of obsessive-compulsive behaviour. One of the symptoms he said was an "unidentified strong persistent feeling something bad was going to happen." He said that and looked directly at me, paused, and smiled a smile that said "I got your number!" He thought I was crazy! I guess not crazy enough to be dismissed as an employee, but I'm sure a note of some sort was attached to my file in the personnel department!

Interestingly, the office for the pharmaceutical company was in Montréal, Quebec, a city obsessed with hockey. The name of the team is the Canadiens. During the training session, the Canadiens were competing for the Stanley Cup playing against their arch rival, the Boston Bruins. The team from Montreal went on to win the cup four games to two. However, after each game that Boston won, it seemed the whole city had—and I quote—"a strong persistent feeling that something bad was going to happen!" I'm sure a mildly obsessive sales representative from Ontario didn't raise too many eyebrows at the time!

After this experience, my search for explanations was primarily directed through books and taking various weekend workshops relating to meditation, metaphysics, energy healing, and personal growth. Even though validation of your personal experiences from others is nice to get, it is not necessary. It is necessary, however, to have that validation from yourself, whatever the experience may be.

Changing Religious Views

As I mentioned earlier, I was raised in a traditional, Protestant churchgoing family. Prayers of protection were said before bedtime. Prayers of thanksgiving and gratitude were said before meals. Sunday school was attended every Sunday morning. My father played the organ for the first service every Sunday. I sang in the youth choir until my voice changed. I had several similar aged friends at church that attended different schools and lived in different neighbourhoods. The only problem was I didn't find the environment inspiring or comforting.

The concept of a "great force in the sky" outside of us, ready to punish if "the word" is not obeyed, didn't sit well with me as a boy. Also, the concept of original sin–that we are created with flaws–didn't make sense to my boyhood logic. As a boy, I liked to make things with Lego type play material. If I didn't like it, I fixed it. If God made man and it was flawed, someone like God would have fixed it long ago, or so my boyhood reasoning told me.

By the time I was an early teenager, my father's pious life had certainly influenced me. I accepted the existence of a supreme being, God. I understood the value of attitudes of thanksgiving and gratitude as well as compassion and kindness. I saw kindness from my Catholic and Jewish friends. I also saw these qualities in other church denominations I attended as a curious middle teenager. I concluded our church did not have sole possession of these attitudes. I appreciated and admired my father's devotion and loyalty to his church and religion. However, by the time I was a late teenager and young man, I had three main misgivings.

Firstly, I did not agree that God could not be reached

directly by any individual. Secondly, I could not agree with the zeal to "save the souls of the heathens." Lastly, of all the different religions, denominations, and churches in the world, how could our church have THE answer, as all others felt they had THE answer?

Firstly, I was told I could not approach God directly. I had to go through his only son, Jesus. My Catholic friends were told they could not approach God either; they had to go through a priest. This concept that God was unapproachable did not sit well with me. Why would an all caring Creator behave like a distant relative or isolated hermit? Why would he have go-betweens? Why would God be a dead-beat Dad? Why would you not communicate with your children? Why did you not want to hear from them until they all were dead? We were expected to pray daily to try and appease this great Master. He held our eternal fate in His hands. Judgement Day cannot be avoided. We needed to pass the test or our eternity would be spent in Hell. Oh yes, watch out for the Devil!

How could the Supreme Creator be so far removed from our daily life? This was a question I often asked myself.

Secondly, souls need to be saved. From the age of nine, I attended summer camp for a week or two every summer. These were church camps. I witnessed many highly emotional, fever pitched, saliva-spitting discussions about how important it was to spread the word of the Lord. If anyone did not receive Him into their heart, they would be condemned to Hell for all eternity. It was our responsibility to "save those souls." When I was growing up, it seemed the entire continent of South America was being invaded by missionaries doing this work. At one camp session when I was fourteen, three young brothers shared their tragic story. They witnessed the murder of their missionary parents by the local people. They were stationed in South America. Their story reminded me of other reports of murder from history classes. The Jesuit priests trying to convert the local people of North America in the eighteenth century occasionally met the same fate. There is a memorial for such a priest close to where I was raised. My dispassionate inner reason told me that if the Truth was being spread, such tragedy should not be happening. Or at least the church should be rethinking their motivations with missionary work. Build schools and water wells. Learn from the indigenous people. Don't destroy their ways of life, traditions, and cultures. I saw this as an attitude of intolerance lacking in respect, kindness, and genuine unbiased concern for others.

At the age of fifteen while at summer camp, I was lured into the forest by a fellow camper. It seemed he was a missionary in training. When we came upon a very private clearing, I was forced to my knees. "Repeat after me," I was told. I gave my soul to the Lord. My public confession happened around an evening campfire a few days later. I was responding to the boots being pushed into my back by my "saviour" fellow camper. This disrespectful attitude was prevalent throughout the camp. I did not wish to cultivate these attitudes in my lifetime. I could not agree with these stances in any way. They also violated Cicero's "mistakes of man," attempting to compel others to believe and live as we do, as quoted in the prologue of this book.

Thirdly, only my religion and church has the right way. This is narcissistic in every way. To embrace such a philosophy is to say only pine trees in the forest can benefit from the life-giving sunshine. All other tress are denied access to the sun. Or, of all the wildflowers in the meadow, only buttercups can receive the benefit of the rain. If the other flowers want the life-giving water of rain, they have to become buttercups. This concept of exclusivity is man made. It has nothing to do with divinity and Spirit. It is ego driven. It is what creates divisions among us. It has been the source of countless wars throughout the ages to current day. Much blood has been spilt in the "Name of God." As a race, we need to cease this senseless violence against each other. I could not embrace a theory that says "Our way is the only way." This lacks tolerance and understanding. I wanted no part of such organizations. I believe we can learn from each other. I have grown to know that religious texts should not be taken literally. They need to be approached as manuals for a joyful and fulfilling life.

I can see where religions—all religions—introduce their members to the concept of something that is beyond what we perceive as ourselves. There is something greater, more magnificent.

My experience by the Bay of Fundy was a direct contact with this magnificence, this Grace. My later Kundalini and out-of-body episodes were also forms of direct contact with God. I received no messages to go out and save the world, only a feeling of incredible joy. There is no exclusivity to my experiences. Half the adult population has reported spiritually transformative experiences.

Currently, I have an unwavering belief in a universal spiritual power that is responsible for all creation, including human beings. I embrace the Swiss psychiatrist Carl Jung's opinion that "religion is a defence against the experience of God." [13] I believe we all have the ability to experience God directly or the divine universal intelligence, or whatever you want to call it. We experience this everyday—we just need to become more aware of it.

My mystical episodes addressed my misgivings about spiritual life as expounded upon by the church. Direct contact with God is our heritage. There is no need to force our religious views upon others, we can learn about our spirituality from each other's traditions. The answer to our existence is that we are all one under one divine spiritual umbrella.

Attitude Towards Healing

October 4, 1972 at about 4 o'clock in the afternoon, I was painting my parents' house. I was in between job contracts. The extension ladder I was standing on suddenly slipped out from under me. I fell to the asphalt driveway where my right ankle crashed into the rung of the ladder. My ankle was fractured, dislocated, and spun around backwards. My leg bone protruded through my skin. The surgeon took two hours to reset my ankle. It took three weeks for the swelling to go down enough for a cast to be set. I returned back to my parents' home for a three-month recovery about November 1, 1972. However, the ankle wouldn't heal. Casts in those days were made of plaster, which deteriorated over 4 to 6 weeks. I would have to return to the hospital for a replacement. An x-ray of my ankle was also taken each time. Nine months passed. There was no healing. My older sister had a friend involved with a spiritual healing group. I decided to sit with her and talk. We exchanged stories of premonitions, the sense of déjà vu and vivid dreams. She counselled me to visualize my ankle as being whole just as I was falling off to sleep. She also said her group would work on me spiritually. After one week of doing this, I felt the bottom of my foot, which had been numb for nine months. The next time my ankle was x-rayed, about three weeks later, that part of my ankle was healed. My attitude towards healing was shifting.

Out of curiosity and a drive to comprehend what had happened to me, I investigated other areas where people were connecting with this energy in a healing capacity. As mentioned in the previous chapter, I started to attend laying-on-of-hands services at a local church.

I also trained to give clairvoyant readings and therapeutic touch. These two disciplines showed me that we are connected individually and collectively to an intelligent, healing invisible force.

I'm now convinced that healing requires a holistic approach. There is an energy component to our human existence that is mostly ignored by Western medicine. Therapies from the East, such as acupuncture, have always worked with meridians of energy within the body. More recently, chiropractic, therapeutic massage, matrix reprogramming, and others are disciplines that adhere to a belief in a naturally occurring healing energy within the human body. These fields approach health and healing from the point of view of manipulating the body to be better physically aligned with this energy field.

Does a cast on a broken finger or an arm or leg do the healing? No, it just aligns the bones so the natural course of healing can take place. We need well trained and competent physicians and health care providers to assess our physical health needs. The physical aspects need to be set in order for the energy flow to be realized.

A young child has the ability to regrow the top of his or

her fingertip if it is accidentally cut off.[14] We have an ability to heal that has not been researched enough. I believe that in a few generations, we will be approaching our health and healing from a very different point of view.

It is my opinion that the emergence of holistic health societies over the past few decades is just the beginning of this shift. Our abilities to heal ourselves in the future will be astonishing by today's standards.

Sensitivity to Electricity, Chemicals and Smells

When microwave ovens burst onto the consumer scene, I started to notice something odd. Every time I stood in front of one that was operating, I would feel in my chest a wave of mildly disturbing energy coming from the oven. If I stepped back about 4 feet, I didn't feel it. I believe this technology has changed as I no longer feel this discomforting energy unless I am extremely close to a microwave.

Whenever I travel in a car and pass very large electrical power transmission lines, I get the sense of an uncomfortable energy invading my being. I feel mildly dizzy and a slight shortness of breath, but it is not debilitating in any way.

Shortly after my first Kundalini experience, I was making a sales call on a medical clinic in a small rural town. It was a Monday and the receptionist was very pleased with herself because the boss finally had followed her advice and had some new carpets installed over the weekend. You could still smell the carpet glue. I complimented her regarding the choice of colour and style she had chosen. I sat down to await my turn to see the physician. After just a few minutes, I started to get a very severe headache, shortness of breath, and also felt very nauseous. I thought I must have eaten something for lunch that suddenly wasn't agreeing with me. I excused myself from my appointment and left.

For the next six months, every time I called on that clinic, I started to feel very ill. I also noticed that whenever I was in a commercial building with new carpets, the smell of the glue would make me feel very ill.

Twenty-five years later, I needed physiotherapy after knee surgery. On a Monday morning, I walked into the clinic. They had new carpets. The familiar smell arose. It took three deep breaths and a headache started. I immediately left the clinic and told the receptionist I had to find a new location, I would not be able to be in that room for at least six months.

These sensitivities appear to be permanent.

Problems with Psychic Abilities

When something within our personal being happens that defies our logic and reason, we seem to either respond in awe or react in fear of the unknown. When we cannot describe something or understand it, we often deny it exists, refuse to acknowledge it, or try to forget it.

When I first started having premonitions, it perplexed me; I didn't understand them and I wished they would simply go away. I reacted to these intrusions of my psyche by trying to ignore them. I tried not to acknowledge these happenings that were popping into my brain. But they kept occurring. I had no control over them. They would appear at random moments with no apparent consistency. One moment I would have a sense of seeing the face of a stranger, and then meet that person a few months later. At another moment I would be sitting at a railway crossing waiting on a train and have sense of a pending train accident. If it happened, I didn't know, as I did not follow up on these types of premonitions. Out of frustration and questioning my own sanity, one day in my apartment I said out loud, "Please leave me alone." Nobody was with me of course! Didn't want anyone to think I was crazy!

Despite my lack of enthusiasm for these adventures, they continued. I got to the point where I eventually accepted it as part of my reality. I basically stopped being perplexed by it all. I became more of an observer of the happenings. I tried to see value in what was occurring. Premonitions of seeing influential people and hearings bits of conversations did give some excitement of anticipation for the future. Premonitions of challenges started the healing process on its way, even though those types of instances were not generally embraced with enthusiasm on my part. My regret is that I didn't keep a journal describing these events over the years—it would have revealed some interesting facts about the "inner life."

I found a copy of the book, The Science of Premonitions, by Larry Dossey MD, shortly after it was published in 2009. This book is invaluable for anyone who is struggling to come to terms with any form of premonitions. Just as the subtitle of the book says, "How knowing the future can help us avoid danger, maximize opportunities, and create a better life." [15] I eventually came to realize premonitions are avenues that Spirit uses to help us. Premonitions are Divine Spirit communicating with us.

I eventually grew to accept and know that we live in two worlds simultaneously: the physical world and the spiritual world. Now I look forward to feeling and seeing premonitions! I enjoy the entire psychic aspect of my existence! I know it is Spirit in action.

More Adventures

My arm is stretched out as far as it can to reach the bottom of this deep hole in the sand I spent the last 15 minutes digging. My fingernails start to claw at the soft clay. In a matter of a few minutes, I have gathered a golf ball sized chunk of clay. Every time I reach down for more, my eyes are level with the sand. I can see the waves of heated air dancing above the sand, the sun glistening off the water, and those marvellous, almost mischievous pinpoints of bright silver dots leaving trails behind them, dancing into and out of the sand to an obviously fast-paced, but inaudible music. I point these dancing pinpoints of silver light out to my sister—all she sees is the sun and the sand.

It made no difference to me—I was seven years old!

I have had the privilege of attending two programs put on by the Chopra Center in San Diego, one in 2011 and the other in 2012. In both sessions, one or two people asked Deepak Chopra what they were seeing when they saw specs of dancing silvery light in their visual perception, just as I had seen. He told us it was prana. This confirmed that there are many people other than myself who have witnessed this phenomenon. In her article "Biology of Kundalini," Jana Dixon explains that "Prana is a Sanskrit word meaning life force ... in Hinduism ... interpreted as the vital life-sustaining force of both the individual body and the universe ... and is the mother of thought and thus also of the mind." [16]

At the age of seven, I was seeing prana, the "vital life" energy mentioned in the Vedic texts. At that age, it was just something going on at the beach on a hot summer day. Today, especially on

35

a dull gray cloudy day, if I gaze at the sky with no focus in my eyes, in a matter of seconds I can perceive this prana dancing and spinning like pinpoints of silvery light appearing as if they were on the top of the flow of gently boiling water.

What is the source of this energy? Where does it come from? Perhaps Creation itself. Nevertheless, it is there; others and I can see it. Is this the source, or conduit, or catalyst, or player in the Kundalini experience described by Gopi Krishna in his quote that I presented in the chapter entitled The Experiences? I suspect it is part of the process.

I know for sure that there is something out there! And not just spinning specs of bright and sparkling light. I had a series of events occur that seemed to indicate the presence of something beyond my logical mind, something that defied reason and explanation. It was as if something unknown was watching over me and protecting me, even from myself. I have been snatched from the jaws of death a few times!

About four weeks after my Bay of Fundy experience, I was in Amsterdam. I was there with a group of high school students all about the same age. We were on a tour sponsored by the Canadian Youth Hostel Association. We were cruising through the canals of Amsterdam and had entered the harbour. Our tour boat was returning to the canal system. The sun was setting; the light was that magic orange glow of sunset. It was being reflected off the water and the ships and made a magnificent sight. I decided to take a photograph. There was a hatch through the roof of the boat, so I opened it, stood up with my head through it, and placed my camera on the roof. I lined up my shot. As the boat was turning to return to the canal system, the image was moving. It was getting better and better. My focus was entirely on this changing image. The light was mesmerizing; it held my entire attention. Suddenly I heard a woman scream and for some unknown reason, I ducked my head just as the boat passed underneath a stone bridge about 6 inches above the boat's roof. I was a fraction of a second away from being decapitated. All I could do was say thank you to the woman who screamed.

Several days later, our group arrived in Arosa, Switzerland.

It was a beautiful clear, sunny day. About six of us took the gondola to the top of Arosa Weisshorn Mountain, which has an elevation of 8700 feet and overlooks the town. The town's elevation is about 5800 feet above sea level. When we reached the top, I immediately left the gondola and wanted to take a photograph that illustrated the elevation as we were now high above the town. I reached the edge of the plateau, I leaned over the edge with no railing for protection (after all, I was a teenager) and took a photo. My front foot was inches from the edge. But suddenly it slipped! I had walked very quickly to the edge, expecting to take my photo and then return to my group of friends. No one accompanied me, or so I thought. As my foot slipped and I was about to fall, a woman from my group grabbed me around the waist and prevented my tumble from the side of the mountain. She must have run behind me as I walked very quickly to get my photograph. I could think of no reason for her to want to follow so closely!

A couple of weeks after my return home from Europe, I was with a friend on a Saturday night walking home from a movie. It was a long walk, so we decided to hitch hike. I held out my hand into the traffic, and my friend window shopped as we walked. We were on the sidewalk engaged in conversation and I only glanced at the traffic if a car slowed. Suddenly, my friend turned abruptly and grabbed me with such force I almost fell over. He pulled me about 3 feet to my left just as a car jumped the curb where I had been standing. The car continued to speed down the road without stopping.

It appeared the jaws of death were after me that summer, yet they missed three times. Three times in three consecutive months—there seemed to be some Guardian Angels or Ooky-Spookies watching over me, influencing other people to rescue me from harm's way. Seven years later, I would survive a car accident that killed the other driver. Something was definitely going on and something was watching out for me, something beyond my comprehension and reason.

A String of Coincidences

After my car accident, I started a downward spiral of self-destructive behaviour. After escaping the jaws of death four times by fractions of a second, I decided to live as if there was no tomorrow. For me, that meant lots of parties, pub gatherings, and nightlife club music. Consequently, after two years, I was still very much alive, but in financial straits. Although I held a real estate license, I was essentially unemployed, in debt, and with no assets.

I had to do something to get my life back on track. An amazing string of events started to unfold when I eventually decided to get myself out of debt and figure out the Ooky-Spookies. I remember that moment. I had just mailed my income tax return—no tax payable as no income meant no tax. I said to myself, "Someday, I want to pay $100,000 in taxes." I had no idea what income I had to be earning in order to pay that amount of tax, but I thought it had to be a princely sum. I was living in a very small apartment with a beehive in the outside wall. I needed a change. Focused on my goals of getting out of debt, paying $100,000 in income taxes, and figuring out the Ooky-Spookies, I looked for work and left the nightclubs behind. Thus began a long series of coincidences.

That was April. By late May, I started a job as a sales representative with a company selling products to medical laboratories. One of my customers was a lady who was listed at two institutions with two different last names and three prefixes, Mrs., Miss, and Ms. This got my curiosity going. It turned out she had just left her husband, started a new job, and was going through some personal transformative experiences. When I was hired by this company, I had been told there were many women working in this field. I was cautioned about any romantic involvement with my customers. If I really wanted to get romantically involved, I was told, do it with competitors' clients, not your own. This lady was not a customer! The coast was clear. I asked her for a date and she accepted. We went out again, and then out of the blue, I was fired. This was November. My friend was going home for Christmas, so I offered to take her to the airport and pick her up after the holidays. Since I was unemployed, I could also look after her two cats while she was away. When she got back from visiting her family, I picked her up at the airport, spent the night at her apartment, and we are still together more than thirty years later.

When we first met, I started to share my premonitions and healing experiences with her. She introduced me to her newfound friends at a meditation group. It was here that I was introduced to Eastern philosophy, the teachings of Gopi Krishna, and the writings of Emmet Fox that I mentioned earlier in this book—what a coincidence! Seven months after the tax return filing, I was on a new path very quickly.

The Ooky-Spookies were starting to make sense. Through universal spiritual law, I could see why some of my life experiences had occurred the way they did. Deepak Chopra, in his book Seven Spiritual Laws of Success, talks about reality being based in pure potentiality. We bring forth our life experiences and happenings through our attitudes, which interact with this energy.

The Swiss psychiatrist Doctor Carl Jung coined the term synchronicity as an experience of two or more events that are apparently casually unrelated or unlikely to occur together by chance, yet are experienced as occurring together in a meaningful manner. [17] Deepak Chopra in his book The Spontaneous Fulfillment of Desire raises the question that synchronicities may be the way that this divine potentiality works to reveal ourselves to ourselves. [18] I now know this to be true.

When I joined my girlfriend's meditation group, I was on a new learning curve about spirituality and how it differed so much from a traditional religious upbringing. One afternoon a member of this group asked if I wanted to join him at a lecture that evening to hear a Native American shaman speak. The speaker's name was Sun Bear. My friend had attended a workshop coordinated by him and even though I had not heard of shamanism, my friend thought I would enjoy the lecture. So I attended. Sun Bear was the chief of his tribe in Washington State. The land they lived on was mountainous and at a high-altitude where weather can be very unpredictable. Every spring, his habit was to meditate on the question of where was best to plant the year's vegetable garden crop. In May 1980, Sun Bear received a message as to where to plant. He and his companions gathered up the seeds and traveled to the location he received in his meditation. When they arrived, it was nothing but a gravel rocky plateau. He checked in again for spiritual guidance and was assured that yes, this was the place. Not believing he was hearing properly, he checked again. How could this plateau, so devoid of soil, be the best place to plant the garden this year? Again, the message was plant here!

So with some reluctance, they went about planting the seeds. Even though both Sun Bear and the members of his tribe were highly sceptical, they followed the advice of spirit. Three days went by and they were all starting to doubt what they had done. Then, on May 18, 1980, Mount Saint Helen's erupted and laid down 6 inches of topsoil on the rocky plateau, covering the seeds with rich, dark soil. The harvest that autumn was the best ever (I used this story in a Toastmasters speech some years later and before giving the speech confirmed the accuracy with the woman who was Sun Bear's wife at the time).

Upon hearing this amazing account about following spiritual direction, I said to myself, "I want to become that sensitive to spirit, to hear clearly the message, and have the faith to follow." I'm still working on that to this day! The one main aspect of the story that escaped my attention for many years was this—Sun Bear had a goal! A dream! A vision! He asked where to plant a vegetable garden!

Was that just another coincidence?

After hearing Sun Bear's speech, reading Gopi Krishna's

autobiography, and experiencing my own out-of-body sensations on the shore of the Bay of Fundy, I knew there was and is a living creative force within the universe. It would still be some time before I realized and knew that it also resided inside my own body. I dedicated myself even more to meditating three times a day. I wanted that connection to spirit! After hearing Sun Bear speak and seeing the action of spiritual guidance and the power of coincidences, my journey involving more coincidences continued. These happenings were coordinated around my goal to pay $100,000 in income tax. Remember, when I set that goal I was very much in debt and basically unemployed. Let's continue to examine these coincidences.

After I lost my job selling to medical laboratories, I quickly got a job in retail sales that didn't pay well, but at least I had an income. I immediately started to send to my debtor very small checks each month, either $10 or $20. This was barely .001 percent of what I owed. The tunnel ahead seemed long, dark, and endless. A few months into my program of paying down my debt, an unexpected angel came forward to pay off my debtor. I continued to pay my payments to my angel; however, they were interest-free. Shortly after that I got my job in the pharmaceutical business, which paid much better than retail. I was able to pay off my debts faster. In what seemed like four very short years, my net worth was finally zero! I was ecstatic to say the least. I would never have thought my debt would disappear so quickly!

Meanwhile, totally unexpectedly, my wife was asked to join the marketing department of a medical laboratory supply company and she did. She was replacing an old acquaintance by the name of Ralph as he was moving on to a company with national responsibilities. About a year and a half later, my wife decided that she wanted to start her own business, with a partner. That was her goal. She didn't specify who she wanted as a partner or what type of business. We started selling Amway products. Six months later, we were driving on the busiest highway in Canada, with 16 lanes of traffic and thousands of cars passing any given point in a matter of minutes. As I was passing a car, I looked to my right and the driver was our old acquaintance Ralph. We had not seen Ralph since my wife had replaced him at that company. We pulled over to the side of the highway and made arrangements to get together for dinner the following week. Over dinner, my wife and Ralph compared notes about the marketing department where she worked. She managed a line of products imported from England, the same job he had held prior to her. They jokingly said they should start their own company and distribute these products since they both knew the contract was up for renewal in five months. By coincidence, Ralph had a holiday booked to England, leaving in two weeks. They put together a marketing plan, proposing to form a new company before he left. Also by coincidence, he would be visiting very closely to the office of this British company. He presented the proposal, which was eventually accepted. My wife had her own business with a partner, the result of several coincidences.

Let's add up these random events. We were driving on a busy highway with thousands of other cars. We passed an old friend, who had a trip to England planned. He would be going to a city where a company would be reconsidering their business plan for Canada. He was one of two people in the entire country of Canada who was familiar with the product line. The other person was my wife.

By the way, when they started their business, I was a silent partner. I was still looking for that $100,000 tax bill!

Ralph had left his job to start their business and I applied for his old job and got it. My salary increased by 33 percent. So did my income taxes–just what I wanted! The next two years were very busy, with my wife working 10 hours a day, seven days a week, and I was flying around Canada, now with national responsibilities. We were busy but enjoying ourselves. Ralph, however, became very ill, and after several false diagnoses, we eventually received the bad news. An inoperable brain tumour was in his brain stem. After seven months of hospitalization, Ralph passed on. For those seven months, my wife assumed his workload. She was at home one hour a day. Coincidentally— yes, another coincidence—I lost my job. I became the house husband doing shopping, cleaning, and cooking. After Ralph's death, we purchased his share of the company from his estate. I went back to work, my wife hired a sales manager, and the business flourished.

Every year, our accountant would calculate dividends to be paid. Each year, they grew. Eventually my income tax payable exceeded my entire gross pay check I was getting from the job that I was doing everyday! Five years later, I paid $108,000 in income tax! I reached my goal! It was the only year I reached that goal. I should have reset the goal, but I didn't.

Let's look back of the many coincidences again. We passed Ralph driving on an extremely busy highway. He and my wife started a company. Ralph passed on. I lost my job. I was needed at home for a while. I became a 49 percent owner of the business. Dividends paid exceeded my annual salary.

By the way, we sold the company for over seven times what we invested into it and retired to a more creative lifestyle of travel, photography, and painting—the results of a lot of work as well as several coincidences!

Throughout those years, meditation and intuition were also involved. At one point, the company I was working for had a particular product that was weak in sales. The accepted wisdom of the day to improve sales was to make more calls, more frequent calls, and more calls to potentially new customers. I meditated on my goal of increasing sales, somewhat like Sun Bear asking where to plant the vegetable garden. The message I received was to stay in the office and not make face-to-face calls—completely illogical! I reduced my travel and stayed in the office more. I started an advertising campaign. We started to field more phone calls inquiring about the product. Our sales rebounded and we had a fantastic year. Unknown to me, this product and its problems were written up in a marketing paper. I received a call from a marketing student asking what I did to solve the problem. She wanted to know what happened in real life, not just the classroom. I did what she and her study group thought should be done, and she was thrilled!

Coincidences and synchronicities are definitely channels through which the Spirit communicates to us individually and collectively. We can also seek direct contact through meditation, prayer, and contemplation. When we listen to these messages and respond to them, our lives become more fulfilling and our dreams and goals are reached and achieved.

Summary

From reading about my out-of-body episodes and Kundalini experiences and the resultant changes and challenges I was exposed to, I would hope you have at least given some consideration to the possibility that part of our human existence is indeed beyond what is perceived by the physical senses. Hopefully, you have considered the possibility that we have a spiritual side to our existence and it needs exploring outside the framework of traditional science and religion.

In any field of human endeavour, we always find people who have different levels of awareness. For example, I was attending a photography workshop a few years ago and one of the participants asked a question that revealed her inexperience. The leader of the seminar, a very experienced photographer, answered the question with ease and clarity. There was no judgment in her voice, as she recognized each participant was at a different level of understanding and skill.

When I was in university, the tutor of my first-year physics class was a graduate student. The student had a professor assigned to him as a mentor. At each level of the physics department, those with more knowledge were sharing what they knew with those who had less knowledge. We see this in all fields of human activity.

How does one become more aware of anything?

We increase our knowledge by concentrating our mental energy on our chosen subject. We think, analyze, devise experiments, and reassess what we have learned and observed as we go along the learning curve. We use our mental faculties. The subject could be photography, quantum physics, public speaking, dance, mathematics, discovering new energy sources, or any human endeavour. We can also seek out teachers and mentors in our chosen field of adventure, either through personal contact or through books written by a chosen mentor.

My mental activity since that summer evening when I was seventeen has been focused on increasing my perception and understanding of the unseen—the spiritual cosmic energy—that I have been experiencing and becoming acquainted with. When I contemplate and meditate, I'm often exposed to new perspectives about the spiritual cosmic reality. When I read books by my chosen authors, I also acquire deeper understanding as ideas expressed by the authors often augment my own observations and experiences or clarify my ideas. Since 2008, I have been keeping a journal as I receive these new impressions. The next sections of this book are a collection of some of these impressions.

PART II
DAILY ATTITUDES

God's Will

The New York Times on April 16, 2012 ran an article called "Surviving a Deadly Twister, Twice in 65 years." On April 9, 1947, Wilma Lake survived a devastating tornado that ripped through her hometown of Woodward Oklahoma. It destroyed more than 1000 homes and businesses and killed at least 107 people. On April 15, 2012, she survived another tornado that again swept through Woodward, this time demolishing 89 homes and 13 businesses and killing six of her neighbours. She survived by standing in a closet in the middle of her home as it was torn apart around her. When it was over, she looked up to see only the sky–the house was completely demolished. Her response, when asked about this happening twice in a lifetime, was "I think the Lord must have left me here for a purpose." [19]

In 1588 during the Spanish (Catholic)–British (Protestant) war, the Spanish were sailing to invade England, with the Pope's blessing for a speedy victory and the return of Catholicism to the British throne. An unexpected storm forced the Spanish to change course. After losing 50 of their 130 ships to the raging sea, there were forced to return home without even putting a foot on British soil. The British were so grateful for the "victory" that they minted a commemorative medal with the saying "Jehovah blew his winds and they were scattered." These winds became known as the Protestant winds. [20] God's Will! According to the British, God favoured Protestant England over Catholic Spain. If you were Spanish, you would have considered it bad luck or evidence of a need to find a more reliable weather forecaster before naval campaigns!

MOMENTS IN TIME | 49

On July 2, 2012, as reported in the Washington Post, President Obama was quoted saying, "Whether it's fires in Colorado or flooding in northern parts of Florida ...We all recognize that there but for the grace of God go I." [21]

God's Will be done! Webster's dictionary defines will as the "power of choosing or determining." [22] Does God choose his favourites during storms or battles? Does God play favourites everywhere he pleases? Does God choose his favourites during sporting events?

On July 25, 2012, BBC Sport ran a story about an Olympian from Trinidad named Jehue Gordon. He was quoted as saying, "I think God has a big role to play in sporting activities, especially when ... things aren't going as well as expected. I think he's the one that can keep you on the ... path." [23]

On February 3, 2008, did God choose his favourite football team? In Glendale, Arizona, the undefeated New England Patriots lined up against the 10 wins-6 losses New York Giants. The Super Bowl is the championship game for American football. The Patriots were 12 point favourites. No team had gone undefeated since the 1972 Miami Dolphins. History would be made again today. It was the most-watched Super Bowl on record with over 97 million TV viewers in the US alone.

New England was ahead 14-10, with 2 minutes 39 seconds left in the game. New York had the ball on their 17 yard line. The Patriots, starting to smell victory, were beginning to congratulate themselves on the sideline. The Giants quarterback Eli Manning, going back to pass on third down, was swarmed by the rushing Patriots team. Miraculously, he evaded being tackled and threw a long desperate pass, which was caught one-handed by an equally desperate, leaping David Tyree. New York went on to win the game. New England's first loss of the season—the championship game! Were the New York Giants God's favourite on February 3, 2008?

We often hear the phrase from survivors of tornadoes, hurricanes, fires, car accidents, or anything that is unexpected and beyond logic, "but for the grace of God, I am alive today. It must be God's Will that I'm still here." Is it God's Will? Perhaps. God's Will always seems to be expressed as something that is outside ourselves, something more powerful, or something that acts randomly—on time for some and not for others. I'm not saying that this does not happen, but let's consider another viewpoint.

God exists within the human experience as well as outside the human experience. In his book, How to Know God, Deepak Chopra states "The 'self' isn't personal ego but a pervasive presence that cannot be escaped … In the third century of the Christian era, an unknown heretic wrote 'If you don't make yourself equal to God, you can't perceive God.' This belief did not succeed as dogma (the heresy here is of course that human and divine are not equal in Christianity) but at other levels it is undeniable." [24]

Imagine, if you will, a world with no human beings, with just animals, plants, rocks, clouds, lakes—all of creation but no people. What would we have? What wouldn't we have?

We'd have the animal kingdom with all its aggression. Yes, animals nurture their young and wolves have been known to show compassion to an injured member of the pack by bringing food to the one maimed. However the lost baby Kudu on the savannah of Namibia Africa would not be helped back to his herd by the hungry lioness—he would be breakfast. We would lose kindness, compassion, understanding, tolerance, forgiveness, celebration, cooperation, love, and caring for each other—all the qualities that make life worthwhile. All those qualities that are honourable and divine, God-like!

Edgar Cayce, the American psychic who lived in the first half of the 21st century, in his readings often referred to mankind as Co-Creators with God. "Spirit is the life, mind is the builder and the physical is the result." [25] The book, The Secret, alludes to this as we attract to ourselves what we think [26]—Co-Creating with God. Spiritual law is created and we access it with our thoughts. Is it not logical that human beings are part of creation and therefore express aspects of this Creation?

In the summer of 2011, a couple of weeks after attending the Chopra Center's Seduction of Spirit program in Whistler, British Columbia, I was sitting in a sandwich shop. As I was eating my lunch, I was deep in contemplative thought about

MOMENTS IN TIME | 51

the meaning of life. Why are we here? Do we just chase after better jobs, rush around between errands, and grab some fast food? I often entertain these ideas. Suddenly, one of those illuminating "Ah-ha" moments of truth flashed into my consciousness. Humanity, collectively, is here to express God, as we are all connected through spirit. Individually we are here to become conscious of this connection and expression!

There were several other people in this sandwich shop. Some were lined up reading the menus on the wall, someone was giving their order to the person behind the counter. Others were eating their lunch at tables scattered around the restaurant. When I had this explosion of insight, everyone stopped what they were doing (whether it was eating, reading, talking, or listening) and turned and looked at me for five seconds! I had not said a word! What a powerful confirmation that we are all part of creation, all connected in some mysterious but wonderfully sacred way!

The Ooky-Spookies had become very friendly!

Is it not logical that participants in the University of Chicago survey, cited in the chapter entitled Spiritually Transformative Experiences, who had spiritual experiences "that changed their lives" are experiencing the activity of Creation? God is part of our nature. Whenever we smile, we are expressing that divine nature. Whenever we are kind and offer encouragement, or caring and charitable in our everyday affairs, we are expressing our sacred selves. We are rising above our self-serving animal instincts. We are expressing God's Will. This is our true purpose in life: to connect with and express the Divine within as we go about our daily routines.

Thy Will Be Done!

The Rules of the Game

Instant replay is either the blessing or curse of modern sport, but it emphasizes that we must play by the rules of the game. Was the player's foot on the line? Did the ball hit the ground? Did the player stay within the boundaries and rules and regulations? We spend many hours as a culture wrapped up in sporting events, always played by a particular set of rules. Sometimes, rules change for the same type of sport. For example in the sport of hockey, European hockey and North American hockey play on differently sized ice rinks. The rules for icing the puck differ. American and Canadian football is played by different rules. There are no fair catches in Canada, no 55-yard line in America, and there is one more player on a Canadian team.

How about Australian football, rugby, or something different? If we get away from professional sports, we get even more variation of rules. No body contact in minor hockey. With house leagues and industrial leagues at sport tournaments, you always get the rules straightened out before you start the tournament. Then there are your pickup games where the rules are set first and then everyone plays.

What are the rules for life and living? Yes, we have laws. Break them and get caught and you will be fined or have your freedom removed by jail time. These rules are diverse, depending upon the cultures you are surrounded by. Spit chewing gum on the sidewalk in Seattle and the only person that cares is the one who steps in it. Spit chewing gum on the streets of Singapore and you get fined. Sell your friend some pot in Canada and you face punishment. Do the same in Saudi Arabia and you may get beheaded.

But what are the rules for life and living from a spiritual perspective? If we can agree that part of our existence is divine, then we have a source for the rulebook.

Have you ever made an error in judgment and then been ridiculed publicly? Have you been on the end of a practical joke that turned out to be very embarrassing? Have you been dismissed from a situation, such as a sudden termination at work or asked to leave a volunteer organization for no apparent, valid reason? Have you ever failed at something and not received encouragement from others to try again? Have you been rejected by a friend for no particular reason? Have you ever felt lost in life, seemingly up against a wall or standing in front of a long, dark tunnel? Have you ever felt completely alone in the world?

What do these challenging examples of life have to do with rules? They demonstrate there are times when our fellow friends and citizens need compassion, tolerance, understanding, patience, co-operation, meaningful communication, and love. These are the divine qualities, the potential which rests within us all that is waiting to be awakened and applied to life situations as they arise. When we express these qualities in our daily activities and when we see situations where they would help the person or people involved, we are playing by the rules.

When we are on the lookout for opportunities to show our divine caring side and exercise those qualities, we are playing the game of life as it was designed to be played. The opportunities are endless. They need not be grandiose or time consuming. We can perform small acts of spontaneous kindness such as holding a door open for someone. Smile at that person whose absent-mindedness caused him to drive his car out of his parking space right in front of you. Put a few dollars in the Christmas food bank kettle. Help a person shorter than you reach that item on the top grocery shelf. Offer encouragement to someone who fell short of their mark. In short, living by that old phrase, "walk a mile in my shoes," will provide an opportunity to play by the rules. Express your divine nature. You will be correct every time. No need for instant replay.

Infancy in Adulthood

Within one hour after a baby giraffe is born, it is running with the herd. It will stay with its mother for nourishment, but it has the ability to take personal responsibility for its movement and interaction within its environment.

I have a friend who is a horseman. He asked my wife and me if we would photograph his week-old foal. We went to his farm and there was an animal very much in motion, alive, and running about the field under the watchful eye of the mare. Who would have guessed it was only a week old.

Most offspring in nature develop very quickly into creatures that can fend for themselves, albeit not as efficiently as their adult counterparts. They develop the ability to react to their environments very shortly after their births. Within three hours of birth, a gray whale calf can keep itself afloat and swim a steady course. It may rest on the mother's back or fins at times until it becomes a strong swimmer; however, the calf responds to its environment very quickly after birth. Nature has planted a very strong survival instinct within its consciousness.

Let's look at human beings from this perspective. As infants, we are totally dependent on other human beings for our survival and movement from place to place. From the moment we are born and for the next several months, we cannot feed ourselves, we cannot walk, and we cannot protect ourselves. We are completely dependent on others. We become psychologically imprinted with the concept that our happiness and survival is completely dependent on other people, who are much larger than ourselves. As we grow and enter the school system, our advancement is again judged by others. We appear dependent on the people in our environment for our very existence. Even as we mature, most of us seek employment from others. Some break this mould and become entrepreneurs. Their success is still gauged by how many people they can convince to purchase their product or service. It appears our livelihood and even our existence as both children and adults is dependent upon others. We seem to have little control over our existence.

Let's examine the situation from a metaphoric point of view, starting with the time just after we are born. In a normal, loving environment, when we are hungry we are fed and when we are cold, we get warm clothes. When we are sleepy, we are put in a place to sleep where we are watched over until we awake. Yes, something bigger is taking care of us—our caregivers, whether they are parents or guardians. They are responding to our needs. This is a very allegorical of our upcoming adult life.

As adults, our desires and goals are attended to by our higher selves, the spirit within, the creative intelligence that exists for all. We need to learn to communicate with this aspect of ourselves, just as we needed to learn physical survival skills as children. When we practise silence, prayer, contemplation, meditation, or train ourselves to listen like Sun Bear, as described in the chapter A String of Coincidences, we are fulfilling our lives as they were meant to be lived. When we watch for coincidences, we are tuning into that spirit, that creative force that generates peace and contentment. We are learning to be self-reliant and self-responsible by tapping into something much greater than ourselves.

I read a book last year called Manifesting Change by Mike Dooley. He suggests, in a very organized manner, just how we might go about addressing the change we want to see in our lives through contact with Universal Intelligence. This can be a challenge, as reflected in a quote he used from Ayn Rand, "the hardest thing to explain is the glaringly evident which everyone else has decided not to see." [27]

We need to become like infants within our adult consciousness and be dependent on something much greater than ourselves. When we acknowledge our relationship with the

Infinite Intelligence within, we will discover the source of our happiness. Embrace the infant within with the intelligence of an open adult mind and tune into your higher self for guidance and protection.

Fear

Fear cuts us off from our divine self. When fear showed up during my first two Kundalini experiences, the light switch went off and the episodes abruptly ended.

    I recently had a dream where I was walking down a narrow path meandering through a wide open, grassy green meadow with low hills. Suddenly, above one of the hills, a lion appeared, then another, and then another. They had striped painted faces like "Tony the Tiger." I suddenly felt fearful. They started to stalk me. I looked around and there were no trees or buildings for protection from the lions. I continued to walk slowly towards them, but my fear would not dissipate. I felt the only safe thing to do would be to lie down in one of the small valleys in the grass and pretend to sleep and hope they would leave me alone. I laid down in the grass. The lions started towards me; I tried not to show my fear. Suddenly, they were upon me and rather than tear me apart for breakfast, they nudged me with their heads and noses. Astonishingly, they started to purr, just like the cats they were. They were treating me like family. I experienced no harm. It seemed I was somehow destined to come across these lions during my walk. Unbeknown to me, a film crew had filmed my reaction to the lions. Upon watching this short movie of myself and my fear, I suddenly felt a great liberation from my fear. I was so overwhelmed by this that I wanted to join the film crew to help them help others to overcome their fears. The dream ended.

    What a wonderful dream to show me the futility of fear.

    I had the good fortune of retiring very early in life. With

the recent changes and slow-downs in global economies and the very low interest rate environment, it has become increasingly difficult to maintain the lifestyle to which we have been enjoying. Consequently, I have been imagining a future with much less income. Fear for the future has been creeping into my consciousness. This dream reminded me that fear is futile. It removes me from the source of inspiration—the divine source—for finding the solutions to life's situations.

How do we handle our fears? Some fear is healthy, especially when trying to cross any street in a major city anywhere in the world. Psychology Today considers fear to be a vital response to any danger, physical or emotional. If we do not feel fear, we cannot protect ourselves from real threats. Psychology Today also states that we often fear situations that are a far cry from life and death and consequently hold ourselves back in life for no good reason. [28]

Robert Puff, Ph.D. suggests trying focused breathing with visualization to address those types of non life-threatening fears, such as the fear of snakes. He also suggests a meditative technique as well. [29] Whether we realize it or not, when we meditate, we are calling on the creative energy within our consciousness for guidance in resolving our situation.

During my third Kundalini experience, when fear came calling yet again, I focused my attention on what it was I wanted, which was to experience the energy as described by Gopi Krishna in his writings. I focused on experiencing the sacred energy as it was being activated within my body. The fear disappeared and the experience unfolded. I focused on the divine within.

Tom Harpur in his book Water into Wine presents a concept that the Gospels and other major religious writings are allegorical and metaphorical, not historical or literal. I agree. In appendix B of the book, he cites some references to fear and how to overcome it. He references the New Testament that says perfect love casts out fear. The Vedic or Hindu version is written as "He who knows that the individual soul … is the Self- ever present within, Lord of time, past and future – casts out all fear. For this Self is the immortal Self." [30] Perfect love and the Self are references to that part of us that is divine, our sacred higher self.

When we begin to acknowledge this divine aspect of our nature and try to live from that space, we will conquer our fears. When we seek guidance from Spirit to achieve our goals and apply our own mental efforts, we will live a more peaceful and fulfilled life individually and collectively. We will all be like a fearless child, eagerly anticipating what will appear around the next corner of life.

We can now see the importance of having a goal or dream in life and bringing in our divine component. When fears and doubts creep into our lives, we need a place to focus our attention, a place to rest our mental activity, a place to calm our restlessness. Do you have a recurring fear in your life? Like my fear of low income. Set a goal or imagine a situation that addresses the fear. For example, I now have an income figure as my goal that I focus on when my financial fears creep into my thoughts. When that happens, I give my goal to my sacred self and forget about it. Easier said than done, but well worth the effort!

Maybe next time, I will pat the lions!

A Swiss Bank Account

Who wouldn't want to have a Swiss bank account?

Those fabled bankers dealing with the superrich on a confidential basis. In the movie The Bourne identity, Jason Bourne, a CIA operative with amnesia, tracks down his Swiss bank account. The bank electronically scans his hand for recognition and he is allowed access to his safety deposit box. There he finds several passports bearing two different names, at least six different nationalities, and lots of cash in different currencies, as well as other items a secret agent would need for his survival.

Yes, a Swiss bank account says you are important and that you have unlimited wealth. The Lear jet is waiting at the terminal when you have finished your business. The staff at the villa will have dinner ready when you return with the new release of Bordeaux. The yacht will be delivered to your vacation place in Monaco next week. We all have our fantasies.

Fantasy or reality? You may not know it, but you already have your own Swiss bank account. Yes, it is confidential, only you can access it, and the withdrawals are unlimited. It does not contain material goods; it contains spiritual goods.

Every action, attitude, and motivation you have directed towards your fellow man and the way you treat people around you are the deposits that you put into your bank account. These deposits are classified by type. For example, were you kind and showing concern for others or being impatience and rude? Whatever, they are stored for future withdrawals. These withdrawals will appear as how other people respond to and treat you. How do you want other people to greet and interact with you as you go through your life?

I would suggest we all want respect from others as well as some encouragement when we trip over our own feet. As well as a little love. A smile or two from time to time would also be nice. This is not too much to ask.

Let's examine your withdrawals.

Do people respect your opinions about issues or do they ignore your positions or even ridicule you? How do you respond to the opinions of others? Do you consider them or reject them outright with little consideration. What deposits did you make?

When you fall short at something, does anyone offer encouragement to you to try again? Do you celebrate other people's failures as if life is a competition, and because they failed, you somehow are the winner? Or do you encourage them to try again? What is available for you to withdraw from your Swiss bank account?

Have you ever had such a bad day that all you want is someone to acknowledge your existence with a smile? When did you last smile at a stranger who seemed to be a little down in the dumps? How many smiles have you deposited so there will be one there when you need one?

As with all good banks, our Swiss bank makes interest deposits into our account from time to time. The deposits our bank makes are different from the ones we make. They are deposits of pure kindness, compassion, tolerance, understanding, acceptance, cooperation and love. Yes, deposits by Spirit are of Spirit. They are there for your exclusive use. The only problem is since we did not put them there, we sometimes don't recognize them when they are withdrawn. If we are very self-centered and usually annoying to everyone around us, we may not recognize when some people respond to us with kindness. Those withdrawals are very foreign to us, but they are available.

We reap what we sow. How we treat others is deposited and filed in our celestial Swiss bank account, waiting to be withdrawn. If you want kind and considerate withdrawals, you cannot get them from rude, self-centered deposits. Our deposits may even be carried over from previous lifetimes.

This may explain why we may be treated with extreme generosity or extreme abuse from time to time. However, just as a farmer cannot get carrots by planting potatoes, our harvest is also dependent upon what we plant as deposits into our Swiss bank account. The unique thing about this bank account is the deposits from Spirit. We can personally add to that file by treating people with respect, concern and kindness. Make only good deposits or the best available at the time, and your life will improve. Your celestial withdrawals will continue to grow and get better and you will enjoy relationships and interactions with others on the level you desire.

Don't you just love your Swiss bank account! Only you can access it!

Look and You Will See

You no doubt have heard "Ask and You Shall Receive." Consider this ....
Have you ever bought a new or new-to-you car? Or have you ever started a new job that included a company car? A model of car you were not familiar with. My first company car was a blue, two-door Pontiac LeMans. I had heard of that type of vehicle; however, I had never noticed them. Until that job, I drove old clunkers or my parents' vehicles. Suddenly, I started to see dozens of Pontiac LeMans daily, all over the highway. It was amazing—where were they all before I started driving one!

In my early twenties, I had a friend who liked to think he was something special. He wanted a car to express his individuality, his unique status (within his mind). I honestly cannot remember what car he decided to buy after a long search. I do remember, however, how shocked he was after he bought it. There were hundreds of these vehicles on the road driven by some strange looking people! His unique car, an extension of his rather large ego, didn't turn out to be as individualized as he had hoped.

I like nice wine—the cheaper, the better! I recently discovered an Argentinean Syrah which I quite like. I found this totally by accident. I thought I was buying a Malbec. The labels were identical except for the name of the wines. I now buy this wine regularly and now notice that it is listed on many wine lists in local restaurants. I had never noticed it prior to my accidental discovery of this particular vineyard.

A few years ago, I was visiting California. I noticed a lot of women were dying their hair with different tones and shades of the same colour. I found it rather interesting and attractive and thought it was very creative. I assumed it was a local hair style. When I returned home, whenever I was in a public place such as a shopping mall or theatre, I noticed many women with a very similar hairstyle. Where were they before my trip to California? I suspect right under my nose, but I didn't see it.

What do new cars, new wine, and seeing different hair styles have to do with understanding our divine nature? When I attend meditation workshops, I often hear people saying, I fell asleep, I can't meditate, or I keep thinking about all those things I have to get done before the sun goes down. They are allowing themselves to be distracted by the familiar routines in their lives. They are not opening themselves up mentally or emotionally enough to let something new into their consciousness. When you entertain the concept of the Divine within and co-creation with this Intelligence, you will start to see this in your environment. It is present in all human beings. You can start becoming aware of this by just smiling. Smile at strangers. Some will smile back, and others will look at you blankly. I started doing this a while ago. I would smile at anyone— it was rather fun. One morning while grocery shopping, a young mother with a small child on her hip walked by me in a hurry. When I saw the child, I smiled at him. He smiled back. I smiled again–and then his face broke into a huge, beaming grin. I suspect I did the same! We saw in each other the Divine Light. I have also had this happen with complete adult strangers while walking in parking lots.

Just like seeing your new car, new wine, and different hairstyles, when you start looking for the Divine in others, you will see it everywhere! It was there all along. When we discover something new or something that appears to be new to us, we realize that it was always in our environment. It was there before we became aware of it, in places we least expected. When you start seeing the Spirit in others everyday, you will also start to see the Spirit in yourself.

Look and You Will See.

Embrace Your Disappointments

I fell in love that summer. She was a blue-eyed redhead wonder of creation. I was not very experienced in matters of the heart; I was downright shy when it came to women! Mustering up the courage, I asked her for an evening date. She accepted!

We spent the summer as young people do, sitting beside the river eating takeout chicken and later watching the waves lapping up on the shore. We spent time together going to music concerts and summer fairs, always talking and getting to know each other. I was afloat on a cloud of near ecstasy for several months. Then it happened. She called and asked me to meet her. She looked gorgeous, wearing a stunning pastel mauve and white dress. She smiled, her blue eyes locked on mine, her mouth opened, and she said goodbye. It was over. Little explanation. The anguish would set in later. At that moment, her words felt like a knockout punch from a heavyweight boxer. I couldn't think of anything to say. I was stunned and emotionally numb. I just left and drove home. It was a long time before my heart opened that wide again.

Two years after my girlfriend left, I received a phone call from the national sales manager of the company I was working for. The man had hired me, but that day he fired me with no explanation. A couple of years later, our paths crossed again and I asked him why he fired me. Still no explanation. The sense of the anguish hit me again.

These two incidences, one personal and one professional, shaped my emotional life. I was forced to contemplate my inner self, my personality. Who was I as a person? Maybe I also licked my wounds a little. Nevertheless, my focus went inward. I asked myself, where was I making mistakes that offended others yet they will not tell me? Or what part of my personality is so offensive that people don't want me around after they get to know me a little bit? Paranoid? Not quite—just concerned! I had the rest of my life to live!

The first answer that appeared in my consciousness was you reap what you sow or what goes around comes around. We get what we give in life. I immediately recalled breaking up with a girlfriend I was with in university, giving her no explanation. I now know how difficult it must have been for her! It had nothing to do with her at all, but I didn't explain myself for my actions. I just walked away without notice.

A second consideration took time to develop.

Whenever we experience disappointments, betrayals, sadness, or situations forced upon us that we find very unpleasant, we are feeling one far end of the arc of a swinging pendulum of emotion. It swings around a neutral central point equidistant on either side. The pain you feel on the one side will be equal to the potential joy you can feel on the other side. I say potential because we do have to do something with our pain. We can wallow in it or seek revenge against those who caused it. We can plot vengeful actions against all who remind us of the cause. We can deny it happened by burying it in our consciousness. Or we can call upon our divine spiritual selves for guidance to address it.

When we call upon our real sacred self, we can see the perpetrators of our pain as sources of inspiration and opportunity to practice applying those higher character traits of acceptance, tolerance, compassion, and forgiveness. When we do this, we suddenly tune into our spiritual nature of calm, joy, and contentment. This creates a push on the emotional pendulum to swing into an equal amount of peace and happiness.

We hear this concept in other ways, such as the idiom "Every dark cloud has a silver lining," meaning you can derive some benefit from every bad thing that happens to you. Marilyn Monroe once said, "Sometimes good things fall apart so better things can fall together." [31] We are not totally aware of where the future takes us, but sometimes we need to leave some baggage behind or change the course of our activities to continue our journey through life. These painful situations are at times such an adjustment.

When we realize our happiness and contentment is in our own hands, we have the freedom to enjoy our lives by adjusting our attitudes and responses to unpleasant issues. We alter our attitudes towards our disappointments by practising acceptance of the situation and when necessary, embracing forgiveness and tolerance.

In an attempt to maintain my relationship with my girlfriend after she dumped me, I would contact her from time to time. She became a student in the city where I lived and her residence was close to where I worked. The last time I saw her was when I drove her to her current boyfriend's place. After dropping her off, I realized she had no interest in me whatsoever, and despite my emotional devastation, I finally accepted the situation and realized my emotional pain was my reaction to her decision. She was not the cause.

A wave of emotional release enveloped me and over time, joy returned to my life—more joy than I had experienced prior to my relationship with her. Upon reflection, my life seemed to be a journey that, after a bit of time, became more cheerful after every setback. The same sense of release and eventual happiness happened when I finally accepted that not every employer will be honest and straightforward with me. The pendulum was swinging at its own soft pace.

I came to realize I don't have to know or understand what motivates the actions of others that I may find unpleasant. The main lessons learned from these two incidents were that I am responsible for my own happiness and peace of mind, and there are divine forces in our lives that are more aware of our lives' direction than our own egos.

Holding on to the frustrations from the past prevents us from seeing the divine pattern in our lives. It also prevents us from experiencing the peacefulness that acceptance of unsettling situations brings to our lives. Embrace your disappointments and accept them for what they are: opportunities to allow the spirit side of your life to flow through acceptance, understanding, and forgiveness. Yes, I fell in love that summer, but the pleasure arrived a little later. Allow the pendulum to swing and ride the wave of joy it will bring you.

Bad Habits

I used to smoke more than 50 cigarettes a day. I eventually quit and then seven years later resumed smoking again. It was two or three a week at first, just when someone offered me one. That was a common social courtesy when I was a young man. Eventually I started to buy my own and within a few months my old habit returned, for 12 years. Then I quit smoking cigarettes again.

I have other bad habits.

In Deepak Chopra's book, The Seven Spiritual Laws of Success, he suggests we "practise non-judgment," as a way to experience the first spiritual law—Pure Potentiality. By doing so, we witness the Intelligence (spirit) in every living thing. [32] Upon reflection of this statement, I realized how easily and quickly I pass judgment on others, especially other drivers on the highway. You know the ones—they cut you off in traffic, run red lights, talk on cell phones as they drive weaving across the lane markings, and park in no parking zones so there is little room for others to get by. You see them, I'm sure. I certainly do. I decided I would try to practise being nonjudgmental. I was in this environment practically every day. I started giving these drivers the benefit of the doubt. They may be talking on the phone as they are driving because they are trying to comfort a loved one after a death in the family. They cut me off because recent neck surgery prevents them from moving their head properly and didn't see me in my lane. Maybe they ran a red light because their child is in the backseat having difficulty breathing and they are rushing to the hospital. Maybe they are parked in the no parking zone because the car stop running there and they're waiting for a tow truck to arrive.

I must admit it was a challenge. I had to stop myself from constantly passing judgment. But eventually I got better at it and didn't let myself get upset by these inconsiderate drivers. Amazingly after a few short weeks, my own demeanour got better. I felt less stressed.

Lately however, I've noticed the stress seems to be seeping back into my life. I also have been noticing and commenting on how many of those lousy drivers are back on the roads this summer!

According to Webster's 1828 dictionary, divorce is "disunion of things closely united;" to marry (figuratively) is "to unite in the closest and most endearing relation."[33] When I was smoking, my habit was indeed married to me in the most endearing way. When I cursed and judged other drivers, my opinions were certainly married to me. My challenge was to disunion things closely united. In others words, divorce myself from my bad habits.

Have you ever overcome an addiction like smoking, overeating, over-drinking, or over-exercising only to fall back to earlier times? We've all done this for sure.

My belief concerning spiritual writings such as the Bible is that they are neither historical texts nor to be taken literally. They are manuals to help us towards comfortable, contented, and peaceful lives, once we understand the metaphors and allegorical stories. They are books of psychology and metaphysics. For example, I lost my job in my early 20s and was feeling very sorry for myself. If a friend called and asked if I wanted to go somewhere, I would always say no. I isolated myself. One day I was looking for advice about my predicament and I randomly opened the Bible to a story about a King. I would often seek advice through spiritual books at that time in my life by focusing on a question or an issue I was seeking a solution to and then randomly open a book for the answer. My favourite books at the time were Emmet Fox books, but for some reason that morning I used the Bible. The King in the story had lost his son in battle. He was so upset he locked himself in his castle and remained there for days that lead to months. No one from his kingdom saw him for a very long time. Eventually, someone from the kingdom got an audience with the King. He explained the King's behaviour suggested he would rather see all of his subjects dead and his son alive. The King realized he was cutting himself off from the joys of his kingdom. He left his castle and embraced those in his kingdom and the contentment it had to offer him. I, jobless, was doing the same. I was allowing one upsetting issue to ruin my life and to remove me from other things I enjoyed. Upon this realization, I became more engaged with my friends and soon found myself working again.

Back to the bad habits! When we stop smoking, try to stop judging others, or attempt to change a bad habit, we are divorcing that habit from ourselves. The Bible gives several references to divorced or "expelled" women, which loosely translate into "don't marry a divorced woman."[34] In metaphysics, reference to female often refers to our inner nature, our feelings and emotions, our attitudes and thinking. Our emotions and attitudes are what drive our habits. Don't marry a divorced or expelled woman means don't re-embrace your bad habits you worked so hard to "disunion" yourself from. Don't marry those habitual ways of thinking and feeling that you chose to throw out and leave behind. When I reverted back to smoking cigarettes after seven years, I was certainly "marrying a divorced woman." Once the desired habit is divorced, move on and enjoy your life.

Another Biblical passage tells us the same thing. As we learn about ourselves and grow spiritually, we are constantly taking new steps along the path of life. We develop new perspectives and awareness of who we are and our relationships to our entire environment. In 1 Corinthians 13:11, we are told "When I was a child, I spoke as a child, I understood as a child, I thought as a child: but when I became a man, I put away childish things." The childish things are our old perceptions, or partially true perceptions that seen in retrospect with new understanding are indeed childish in a metaphoric sense. Childhood always precedes adulthood, no matter what the chronological age.

We can also compare this concept to climbing a mountain. When you reach the peak, you can see another mountain in the distance. While climbing the first peak, you are leaving childish things behind as you make your ascent and become the adult when you reach the peak. With your new perspective, you see the next peak, and the adult is suddenly a child again climbing the second peak.

We also see this in our physical lives. We start as a dependent child, become an adult, and for some, age into a dependent "child" again. Giving up childish things and not marrying a divorced woman are both telling us to keep moving forward in our search for truth and understanding about ourselves. Once the bad habit is left behind, leave it there.

If you are feeling adventuresome after your successes, you may want to look for other divorce material or change your perspective on other issues in your life.

Are you living your adult life from childhood perspectives? As an adult, I went back to my childhood home and looked at the huge hill we had in our front yard. It was three feet high! When you are 18 inches tall, 3 feet is huge! Are there beliefs from your childhood that need to be examined from your adult perspective? Have you embraced the prejudices of your upbringing? Sometimes our divorce material rests within our psyches and is difficult to see without honest reflection. As we grow our perceptions and understandings change, we put away childish things and we are constantly divorcing the past. The phrase "don't marry a divorced woman" reminds us to keep it that way. It reminds us that life is a forward moving adventure. Leave the cigarettes behind.

Sometimes the divorce material seems endless! But it can be liberating!

Creating Gifts

Mahatma Gandhi has been quoted as saying, "Be the change you want to see in the world." Some feel he did not actually use these words, but they are a paraphrase from one of his 98 volumes of writings. In Volume 13, he writes: "We but mirror the world. All the tendencies present in the outer world are to be found in the world of our body. If we could change ourselves, the tendencies in the world would also change. As a man changes his own nature, so does the attitude of the world change towards him. This is the divine mystery supreme. A wonderful thing it is and the source of our happiness. We need not wait to see what others do." [35]

Thoughts are things. From the writings of James Allen and Prentice Mulford in the late 1800s and early 1900s to Rhonda Byrne, author of The Secret published in 2006, we have been exposed to the concept of how our attitudes affect our lives. Napoleon Hill in his book Think and Grow Rich goes into great depth analyzing the relationship between attitude and wealth. [36]

Charles Fillmore, founder of the Unity Church, says "thoughts are things ... The mind of man marshals its faculties and literally makes into living entities, the ideas it entertains ... the word 'things' expresses ... our creative thoughts ... and the marvellous ability of our mind in its creative capacity." [37]

In his book, The Divine Matrix, Gregg Braden cites studies from 1972 when a specific number of people meditating in various Americans cities seemed to influence the entire population of that city in a positive fashion. Violence declined during the meditation periods. Similar studies from the Middle East in the early 1980s found comparable results. There was a reduction in crime, terrorist activity, emergency room visits, and other violent acts during periods of meditation. When the participants stopped their practice, the statistics reversed. It was concluded from these studies that the minimum number of meditating people required to "jump-start" a change in social group consciousness is the square root of one percent of a population.[38]

When I was a university student, I worked for a local conservation authority in the summer. We were transforming a 640 acre farm back into its original natural state and creating a forest. Thousands of trees were planted over two summers. A dam was built across the creek and a small lake appeared. We trucked in sand to create a beach. Roads were built so park visitors could travel between the camping area and other areas of the park.

Forty years later, I visited this park. I watched people walk their dogs among the trees; it was now the forest we had envisioned. Children were playing on the beach. People were playing soccer in the open areas. The old change house had been renovated. Something I had done four decades earlier was being used and enjoyed by many people today. Even though it was only a summer job, the saplings I spent many hours planting were my gifts to the regeneration of the forest.

What do a statement from Gandhi, thoughts are things, the square root of one percent of a population, and planting trees as gifts have in common? Taken together, they are symbolic and metaphoric of life.

When we acknowledge our spiritual side and accept that divine creation is an integral aspect of our human existence, we now have a choice. That choice is to apply that knowledge by being less judgmental, more tolerant, more understanding, and expressing more concern for others. These attitudes reflect the divine spiritual side of us. These attitudes are similar to the saplings I planted—gifts to be shared. When we adopt these attitudes as our thoughts, our thoughts become things: spiritual entities of kindness, tolerance, understanding, and acceptance. These become gifts that are available for others to use and experience. Yes, our thoughts become "things" in the spiritual realm and influence those around us as evidenced in the meditation experiments of the 1970s and 1980s. How this works and is applied is a mystery, but it works! And it takes very few people to see an influence.

When we express our spirit, these divine qualities are being generated like an electrical power plant generates electricity. The power is not selective; it is available to everyone, although we need to make the choice to plug into it. When we express our spirit, we are contributing to the betterment of mankind because our thoughts of compassion and generosity are being generated and made available to all. The meditation experiments cited by Gregg Braden demonstrate how these gifts influence even those who do not embrace compassion but embrace violence.

We are becoming the change we would all like to see in the world, a world of kindness, harmony, more concern for others and free of violence. Embrace your spirit, express those qualities, and generate those gifts.

PART III
UNIVERSAL ENERGY

A Subtle Impulse

What is an altered state of consciousness? According to the Merriam Webster dictionary, it is "any of the various states of awareness (as dreaming sleep, a drug-induced hallucinogenic state, or a trance) that deviate from and are clearly demarcated from ordinary waking consciousness." [39] According to Wikipedia, it is also called an altered state of mind and is "any condition which is significantly different from a normal waking beta waves state." [40]

What is a beta waves state? It is the most active of the four types of brain waves. Anything below that is considered altered, whether naturally induced such as going to sleep or relaxing or artificially induced by drug use. The UN Office on Drugs and Crime was referenced in an article by the CBC on June 24, 2009 titled Illegal drugs: Canada's Growing International Market. It was estimated that for the global age group of 15 to 64, there were 200 to 304 million active users of the top five illegal drugs—ecstasy, cannabis, heroin, cocaine, and amphetamines. [41] That is approximately equal to the entire population of the United States! (314 million people in 2012). Or eight times the population of Canada, which was 35 million in 2013. According to the Centers for Disease Control and Prevention in 2010, 12 million Americans used prescription painkiller drugs for non-medical reasons. [42]

The Health and Social Care Information Center in England reported in 2010 that 68 percent of men and 54 percent of women had consumed alcohol in the week prior to their survey. [43] A Gallup poll conducted in July of 2012 found 66 percent of

Americans used alcohol with 44 percent having had a drink in the week prior to their survey. [44] The National Institutes of Health reported there are approximately 18 million Americans considered alcoholics or having an alcohol problem. [45]

Let's look at a relatively harmless substance. Coffee, containing caffeine, is consumed by 83 percent of Americans on a daily basis, an increasing trend. [46] Energy drinks, which also contain caffeine, had sales totalling $12.5 billion in 2012. [47] Caffeine is not a new problem. Gourmet coffee zone reports that caffeine addiction was considered a social problem in the 18th century in Europe. [48]

Addictions are not the sole property of today's society. Addictive substances go back even further than the 18th century. For example, opium has been referred to for centuries and was actually cultivated in Egypt in 1300 BC for export to neighbouring countries. [49] Opium continued throughout history to be used in all areas were humans congregated. How do we define addiction? Time magazine, in an article called "Hooked On Addiction," defined it as "compulsive behaviour related to a substance or activity that people continue to engage in despite its negative consequences." [50]

According to researchers, some non-drug associated addictions such as to food and sexual activity are often linked physiologically to substance addiction. However, not all addictions involve the human body's pain-pleasure response. Some people are addicted to video games, the internet, exercise, shopping, work, or gambling. [51] [52] Some are addicted to self-improvement. Yes, some people don't feel satisfied unless they are continually taking night school courses, correspondence courses, online courses, or any other intellectual or self improvement pursuits. I recently attended a Toastmaster convention where a member was honoured for achieving 12 educational awards over the past 12 months. In order for the member to achieve that, he would have had to attend a Toastmasters meeting almost every waking moment of his life. He would have had to eat and breathe the Toastmasters program 24 hours a day, seven days a week for the previous 365 days. If he was involved with cocaine to that extent, he would be labelled an addict.

Addiction is a complex issue. Much research has been done and continues to be done in seeking to understand the balance between pleasure and self-control. However, these behaviours seem to me to point towards the existence of a search for contentment and personal peace. It appears humanity has been searching for a very long time. We seem to have a constant irritation that is propelling us towards a different mental state than our normal waking state: an altered state of consciousness.

Addictions are not the only way mankind has pursued this search for altered states of consciousness, this escaping the beta waves state of normal wakefulness. Meditation has been referred to in literature since antiquity. Most religious traditions since the early Vedic times of India have rituals involving mental concentration. The Buddhist Center describes meditation as a means to transform the mind: in other words, a search for altered states of consciousness. [53] Surveys done in 2007 by the National Center for Complementary and Alternative Medicine in the United States (the latest data I could find) found 20 million people meditated, a 25 percent increase over the previous five years. [54] If we extrapolate the numbers, the estimate for 2012 will be 25 million people now meditating. They did another survey in 2007 and found 2.3 million Americans practised Tai Chi, another form of mental concentration involving a specific series of controlled body movements. [55] I find it interesting that meditation, or some ritualistic form of mental concentration, has been practiced by mankind for as long as mankind has been smoking opium!

If we look at global drug use of today, the wide variety of non-substance addictions and the increased interest in meditation and other forms of mental concentration, especially in the Western world, we see a pattern in human behaviour that suggests a drive towards an altered state of consciousness. There is a search for deeper feelings of calm, relaxation, and emotional bliss. This would suggest a response to an impulse, a spiritual impulse, within us, just like the drive for food and sleep. This spiritual instinct is pushing us to experience states of existence that are beyond our normal waking state. Since the beginning of time, we have developed tools to address this impulse. These include all forms of mental concentration. Religious rituals, self guided meditations, and related physical activities such as Tai Chi are all forms of mental focusing. Then there is the express route—drugs. However, this route is very troublesome and can lead to self-destruction. I believe mankind individually and collectively needs to acknowledge the existence of this spiritual impulse. We need to realize we are part of this divine creation. By coming to this understanding, self-destructive drug induced behaviours and other addictions would lessen.

When we acknowledge this impulse as an integral aspect of our human nature and work with it as part of our own experience, our cultures and societies both individually and collectively will thrive. We would experience more calm, goodness, and peace. We must, however, first acknowledge the divine spark within ourselves and nurture that understanding to its fullest. When we do this, we will be on the road to allowing our instinctive altered state of consciousness to occur in a natural and blissful way.

When our bodies need food, water, and sleep, we respond to these instincts by eating, drinking water, and resting. We are soon satisfied in a pleasing manner, and our calm returns. When we recognize our sacred impulse and respond and address it appropriately, our calm will be coming from a much deeper center within our being. We can nurture this inner impulse through such activities as meditation, focused thought, increasing our respect for and spending time in nature, and contemplation.

Another method of nurturing our divine side is focusing our thoughts on creative activity.

Creativity

Are you creative?

When asked this question, I often hear people say, "I can't draw a stick man!"

Creativity is not just related to art, writing, or music.

We are not all destined to be the next Picasso, Shakespeare, or Mozart.

Creativity involves any activity where we apply our intelligence, try something new, and create something that didn't exist before, whatever those endeavours may be.

When we were toddlers, learning to walk and talk, we were being very creative. We discovered falling down did not work, so we analyzed and adjusted our footsteps and tried something new. We did the same with talking when we exclaimed "No one understands me!" We said it differently and eventually something new was created and people understood as expected. A conversation was created. We followed this path of learning and creating until we mastered walking and talking, trying something new at each step on the way. That is one way creativity works.

Whether we are learning a new language, learning to play a musical instrument, painting our first painting, rewriting a marketing plan, changing the way we are raising our children, or changing our habits, we are drawing on our creative, divine spark for guidance, inspiration, and expression. The energy becomes closer to us, and as a result, we gain other benefits besides doing something differently and more effectively.

Let's take a look at the life of Michelangelo. He was an

Italian sculptor, painter, architect, and engineer. He is one of the few artists who had biographies written about them before they died. Throughout his life, he was often referred to as Il Divine (the divine one). His statue of David was crafted just before he turned 30 and still stands in Florence, Italy today. He was commissioned to paint the ceiling of the Sistine Chapel at the Vatican in Rome, a work of art still admired by millions almost 500 years later. At the age of 74, he took over the design of St. Peter's Basilica. The world famous dome of the Basilica was the creation of Michelangelo. His life was a prolific string of creativity, not just self-driven but also commissioned by the Catholic Church in Rome and the Medici court in Florence. His name is synonymous with the High Renaissance era.[56]

Michelangelo was born March 6, 1475 and died February 18, 1564. He lived to be almost 89 years old. During that era, the average life expectancy was approximately 40 years. The noble class of the time tended to live about 10 years longer and some did live to be 60 or 70. He lived almost twice as long as his average countrymen!

Putting that into perspective, it is like a man living in North America today surviving to the ripe age of 152 (twice the life expectancy in 2010 of 76 years). This is of course a bit far-fetched, yet many people today are living past one hundred years. Living to be 152 is highly unlikely even with all the magic of modern medicine. How did Michelangelo live so long when medicine was far more primitive than it is today? Just the lack of antibiotics alone would keep the global population in check for many centuries.

Let's add more perspective to the phenomenon as to how his body managed to survive the harsh realities of his time in an almost miraculous manner.

Michelangelo toiled under at least seven Popes, the first being Julius II. No doubt the Popes would have been provided with the finest foods and best medical expertise available during their reigns. During Michelangelo's lifetime, the youngest Pope, Leo X, died in 1521 at the age of 45. The oldest Pope was Paul IV, who died in 1559 at the age of 83. For all the Popes in his lifetime, the average age of death was 65.3 years. He lived about

38 percent longer than the average Pope and almost twice as long as Pope Leo X. [57]

Let's look at another famous Italian of the Renaissance era, Galileo. Galileo was born three days before Michelangelo died. Galileo's greatest invention was the telescope. He was able to observe moons orbiting the outer planets. Through these observations, he concluded correctly that the sun was the center of the universe, not the earth, as the Roman Catholic Church preached. He was condemned by the church and spent the last several years of his life under house arrest. Despite his highly creative life that clashed with the ruling elite of the time, he still lived for 78 years, longer than most Popes of his generation.

Eleven months after Galileo died, Isaac Newton was born. This astronomer, mathematician, and scientist changed the way mankind understood his world. He was another highly creative individual who lived a long life (83 years) at a time when the average life expectancy was barely 40 years.

In my humble lifespan, during the years I dedicated myself to meditating three times a day, I never caught a cold or flu. Meditating regularly brings divine energy closer to us. We are always in contact with this energy, but consciously making a choice for contact brings it closer. By choosing to mediate regularly, I was actively engaging with the creative force, the divine essence within. It brought me that healing and protective nature that is inherent to its nature. I believe this is not unique to my experience but is available to all who practise meditation or engage in creative, thought-focused activity. Creating anything involves concentrated thought.

Not all artists and creative geniuses in history have lived twice as long as their peers. However, I believe the possibility of a link between creativity and longevity merits some consideration in the cases of Michelangelo, Galileo, and Isaac Newton. By being extremely creative and almost obsessed with their passions (Michelangelo slept in his clothes and boots), these men extended their lives well beyond the standards of their times and well beyond the privileged of their eras. They appeared to live a life of almost total concentration on creative projects during every waking moment.

Being creative draws this divine energy into our lives, a protective and healing energy. You do not have to pick up paint brushes or sculpting hammers to be creative. Change your favourite bread recipe or discover a new path for your usual walk through your local forest or park. Change your daily routine. Read a different genre of book. Creativity is not just art, writing, or music; it happens whenever we observe our life experience and apply our intelligence and imagination to bring about changes for the betterment of our lives.

Be creative in any way—it may be the best medicine yet!

Mirror Mirror

We human beings manifest our thoughts and attitudes. We are natural expressions of energy —it cannot be stopped. It is our nature. How can we describe this process? In the book As a Man Thinketh by James Allen, there is a short poem that ends with these words: "we think in secret, it comes to pass, our environment is our looking glass." [58]

Let me explain this passage. We think in secret—our thoughts are generated within ourselves, our personalities, our bodies. It comes to pass—these thoughts are like magnets when acted upon by the Universal Energy and appear in our surroundings. Environment is our looking glass—our physical surroundings mirror our dominant thoughts and attitudes, just as nature designed us! We cannot escape this because it is who we are.

Would you like to know yourself better? Look around—objectively! What types of people surround you? Are they argumentative and self-serving or helpful and tolerant? Do they listen intently or constantly interrupt you? Are they somewhere in between these extremes? Most of us are. Watch the people that come and go in the groups that you belong to or the businesses you frequent. Observe the dominant characteristics of their personalities, not the minute-to-minute expressions. You will have to be very honest with yourself, and at times you will have to take a leap of faith. It can be fun and rewarding to see how you change and grow by observing the people that are attracted into your life.

I remember resenting people who were always trying to

force their ideas on me, until I noticed myself doing the same from time to time! I had a co-worker once who was very impatient and extremely self-defensive. If you made a suggestion to him about doing something a little differently, you were greeted with a verbal barrage as to why his way was best. Even days later, he would still be reminding you. After one particularly trying day on my way home, I told myself I was glad I was not like him. I was open to suggestions about how to improve myself and go about my day to day activities. After dinner that evening, I was putting the dishes away and my wife mentioned it would be easier for her if I put the small plates in front of the big plates. I immediately started to tell her how my way was best, just the way my co-worker would tell us why his way was best. I realized "my environment is my looking glass!" I decided to try and curtail my lectures to others when they offered suggestions. I started to listen more. I soon found I was less stressed with other people's opinions.

Two things are very important when you do this type of self-examination. Firstly, do it objectively, not in a self-judgmental way. Secondly, call upon that divine spark within and treat yourself to your own consideration and patience. Want to go deeper? Let's try.

What else is in our environment that we all can see?

Most mornings, my habit is to read first thing and meditate later in the morning after breakfast. One morning after reading Gregg Braden's book The Divine Matrix, I approached my meditation with a sense to mentally re-visit a photography trip my wife and I had taken to Yellowknife, Canada. We were there to photograph the aurora borealis (northern lights). The best time to see the lights is between 11:00 o'clock in the evening and 3:00 o'clock in the morning. We went during the new moon in January, and the air temperature was close to minus 40 degrees Celsius (and Fahrenheit). At that temperature, you leave your car running all night so it will not freeze up and leave you stranded. I recalled peering into the silent night sky, seeing millions of stars. They appeared to be sparkles of light like pinpricks through a deep bluish black material with a huge powerful light behind it. The sky seemed endless and appeared to stretch out to infinity. I realized some of the stars were light years away and some no longer existed even though we were now just seeing the light they were reflecting. Then the predominantly minty green northern lights started to dance across the dark sky like shimmering lace curtains being blown by a gentle breeze through a partially opened window. I could almost sense the energy like I did with my Toastmaster friend and while visiting the Bay of Fundy. It was extremely awe inspiring!

I then realized, in my meditation, that I was looking into the mirror of my creation, myself, and my being. My environment is my looking glass. I am a part of this wonderful creation. I am Infinite! We are all infinite!

I felt a shudder of excitement engulf my entire being that morning. A shiver ran up my spine. My hair stood on end. A wave of joy crashed over me. If I had not been sitting, I would surely have fallen over. It took my breath away!

Yes, this is who we really are!

Natural Healing

On June 22, 1969, the Cuyahoga River in Cleveland Ohio caught fire—yes, a river burned! It was so badly polluted with oil laden debris that a passing train throwing a spark from its wheels caused the river to ignite and burn. Even though the fire barely made the local news, it was reported in Time magazine several weeks later and became an environmental rallying cry. This eventually led to the creation of the Environmental Protection Agency and the Clean Water Act in America. [59] The Cuyahoga River empties into Lake Erie, the shore of the lake in which I dug for clay and watched the prana dancing in and out of the sand. I remember watching Lake Erie nearly die due to the extreme pollution of the post World War II industrial era. In 1969, Neil Armstrong walked on the moon, Woodstock happened, and a river was polluted enough to burn. What happened to the river?

It took some time, but 40 years later, people kayak down the river, fish survive, and parts are fully restored. How did it happen? Firstly, a new social respect for the environment had to emerge. The citizens of Cleveland eventually voted to tax themselves $100 million towards the river cleanup. The Ohio Regional Sewer District spent $3.5 billion in the redesign and handling of pollutants. Local governments removed dams that trapped pollutants. [60] Although not fully restored to its natural beauty, something that is most likely impossible, the river is symbolic of what can happen when we choose to cooperate and co-create with nature. When we allow nature to take its course, it heals and restores. That is its power, character, and essence, re-establishing balance naturally.

When we become aware of the spiritual divine aspect of our human nature and allow its expression through our individual tolerance, kindness, and unselfishness, our personal stresses and discomforts will lessen, even possibly disappear, or at least have little hold on us in a negative sense.

Psychologists and therapists often prescribe volunteering to their patients—why would they do that? This gets them into the divine energy flow of caring for others in a small way, expressing the compassion that is naturally present within us. When they engage with others with this attitude, their symptoms of stress and discomfort lessen or become more manageable. That healing flow that we saw in nature with the Cuyahoga River also flows within ourselves, as we are also part of this creation. When we stop polluting our physical environment, nature heals it for us. When we stop polluting our inner environment, the divine energy will re-balance our lives personally and collectively. We do this by reducing or eliminating selfish ego-focused attitudes and adding more cooperation, and consideration for others to our consciousness. As we start to focus on this divine aspect of our existence, our own personal discomforts, such as fear and anxiety, will start clearing up and fading away. We will experience more peace, calm, and contentment within ourselves. We will feel more of that divine love and joy that resides within our existence. We will be healed naturally, just as a badly polluted river in Cleveland returned to its natural state once the pollutants were eliminated.

Abundance and Expansion

I believe if we observe nature, we will see our own lives reflected back to us, metaphorically.

I like being in nature. I once had a job working in the forest. Using a specialized tool, we would randomly bore into the trunk of a tree. We would extract a small sample of wood just a few millimetres wide. We would then count the rings on this core and determine the age of the tree. Some rings were wider than others, a reflection of environmental conditions of the year. Yet every year, the tree grew and expanded. Every year, that same tree also produced hundreds if not thousands of seeds. The creative energy being expressed through a tree is both expansive (growth) and abundant (thousands of seeds). A tree does this by just being a tree, the way nature made the tree.

If we allow ourselves to reflect on this fact metaphorically and embrace the concept of expression through expansion and abundance, we can see this happening in our own lives, particularly when we pursue our goals, dreams, and desires. Even though I wasn't aware of it at the time, my attitude shifted when I wanted to pay $100,000 in income taxes (the seed) from an attitude of lack to one of abundance. Unknowingly at the time, I mentally tuned into my real spiritual self and the dream began to grow, not unlike the seed from a tree. Once a tree seed is planted in the earth, nature takes over. When we set a direction in our lives by deciding what it is we want to accomplish and achieve, the Universe treats that decision like a planted seed and gets to work. We cannot physically see this, just as we cannot see what is happening to the seed planted in soil. But nature has now taken over.

We need to nurture the tree seed by watering and weeding. The seed in our mind that is our goal must be also nurtured. When we have doubt and fear, our desires will not materialize. These are the weeds that creep into our consciousness and we must remove them. We replace them with hope and faith and a reconfirmation of our desired goal. The garden that is Creation takes over once we decide which seed we want to plant.

I believe all religious texts are manuals of psychology, metaphysics, and guidelines for successful living if we take the time to study the metaphors. There is a phrase in the Bible from Genesis verse 9:7 that says (paraphrasing), "Go forth and multiply... in the earth." This is a revelation of our expansive nature. When we actively and wilfully "go forth", in other words, decide what our goals and desires will be, the Universe responds to this activity with abundance, "multiplying." That is its nature, and our results (our desires) appear here in our earth environment.

By responding to the desires that rise up within us and following them, we can set the direction of our lives. We can determine what it is we wish to be in this life. We determine what we wish to accomplish. We are like the tree; we are engaged with this creative force. Our heart guides us, our minds set the target, and the Universe responds with abundance and expansion.

More Abundance

During the month of November 2012, the Chopra Center in Carlsbad California presented a 21 day meditation challenge. This was an online program that you could take in the comfort of your own home. These challenges are a regularly offered by the Center to anyone interested in meditation. This challenge was called Creating Abundance.

Day 12 of the program was entitled Abundance and the Law of Intention and Desires. The program started with a quote from Carlos Castaneda: "In the universe there is an immeasurable indescribable force which shaman called intent, and absolutely everything that exists in the entire cosmos is attached to intent by a connecting link."

We were told that attention energizes and intention transforms. When you plant the seed of your intentions into the "field of all possibilities," the universe; the right people, situations, and circumstances will be attracted to you.

Before the meditation started, we were asked "What do you want?" Then we were told to visualize our intention and write it down. When we entered meditation, we would release it to the "infinite organizing power of the universe." The guided part of the meditation had us visualize, putting our intention into an imaginary bottle. We then sealed the bottle and standing by the edge of the ocean, which represents the cosmic divine energy, we threw the bottle into the ocean. This symbolically had us planting the seed of our intention into the soil that is the cosmic conscious "field of all possibilities."

In my meditation, the moment my bottle hit the surface of

the ocean, a pod of dolphins appeared. They were very playful, jumping out of the water and creating a lot of splashing. They took my bottle of intention and tossed it among themselves like a beach ball. They got very excited swimming back and forth. Eventually one of them tucked it under his fin and they swam away. As they left, it was communicated to me that my intentions are commands of joy for the Universe. They would start working immediately on my intentions. More splashing and squeals of delight followed as they left my inner field of view.

What wonderful dreamlike imagery to show the relationship between our desires and how they are achieved! We assume our accomplishments are the sole result of our own effort, but what about those unexpected events that happen along the way to achieving our desires? Where did they originate? What about those co-incidences? During the time this meditation challenge was running, I was re-examining writing this book. My intention was to complete the book. I had sent a book proposal to a publisher in October, but it was not accepted. A nonfiction book proposal only requires a few chapters to be written, not the entire book. Restarting the project was my intention. I decided to completely finish writing the book before seeking out another publisher.

That fall, I was at a Toastmaster convention and unexpectedly a friend asked if I wanted an accountability buddy for any projects I might have underway. An accountability buddy is someone you contact at a regular agreed upon time frame to help in accomplishing your goals, to help keep you on track. My friend had not planned to find a buddy prior to the meeting. Neither was I was looking for such an arrangement. He just blurted it out in conversation and we then considered the concept. I was not putting much time into my book project. This would certainly help. He had some pressing issues as well. It seemed like a good idea. We decided we would contact each other weekly and monitor the progress of each other's projects. Over the next several months, I must admit that had I not had to "report in" that week, I probably would not have done any work on my book. This was a coincidence. However, I believe I could hear dolphins swimming nearby.

A few weeks later, the publisher I submitted my book proposal to announced an online course for learning the steps required to publish in today's environment of social media and electronic imprints, such as Kobo and Kindle. I signed up. The dolphins were swimming closely again.

When the first draft of this book was completed, I decided to start to look for a publisher. There are many available with varying options and requirements; it can be a daunting task for a new author unfamiliar with the publishing world. I spent many hours online looking at various publishing options. I discovered there are huge publishing concerns that turn out self-published books like machine guns aimed at nobody in particular. I found companies that appeared to concentrate on a specific genre of books. Then there is the distribution aspect—do you create an eBook or a printed book or both? It was all a spasm of information jumping all over the internet. It was very confusing. When I contacted one publisher, within three minutes after the beginning of our first phone conversation, the person on the other end of the line actually asked if I was willing to go on a speaking tour to promote the book. Of course I was! I am a Toastmaster! However this seemed rather unrealistic to me since I had not published a book before. I was an unknown potential author. I kept on investigating other more down to earth options and found a couple of publishers that seemed to be more realistic.

During that time, my wife visited a new business networking group. There she met a woman who had just self-published a book a few months earlier with one of the publishers I was considering. We met over lunch the following week. We discussed her experiences with this publisher, both her positive adventures and issues that were disappointments. After our conversation, I decided I would go with the publisher she used. The dolphins were splashing about again.

When we are aware of the relationship between our goals and our spirit, we need not doubt the outcomes. We must keep doing what we feel is appropriate to accomplish our goals and at the same time watch for the coincidences involving people and situations that the spirit is presenting to us. Life is not random. The dolphins are swimming, responding to our intentions with squeals of delight all along the way.

Deepak Chopra states everything that happens in the universe begins with intention. When you decide to buy a birthday present, wiggle your toes, or call a friend, it starts with intention. And intention is a directed impulse of consciousness that contains the seed form of what you wish to create. Like real seeds, intentions cannot grow if you hold onto them. Only when you release your intention into the fertile depths of your consciousness can they grow and flourish. [61]

Set your desires and dreams and then release them to the Universe. Let it work for you. Believe and know that something greater than yourself wants you to realize your dreams. It is offering the guidance and suggestions you need to act upon and pursue to bring your desires to fruition. Watch for coincidences and unexpected developments and follow where they take you. Listen to the people or situations that spirit is bringing into your life. Why not put your efforts in the best places possible? This is what the Universe is giving you. Do that and let the abundance appear. Is that splashing I hear?

The Food Buffet

When my wife and I were working, my office was an hour commute from our home and my wife's office was less than a half an hour commute. On the days she decided to work late, on my way home we would meet for dinner at a Chinese buffet restaurant two blocks from her office. This restaurant had over 100 items on its menu, not only Chinese food but Western, Italian, and Mexican food as well. You could dine at this Chinese restaurant and not eat any Chinese food! It was very popular, especially among people with children. Whoever heard of a Chinese restaurant that served pizza and tacos? I would usually take a variety of dishes: always a sweet-and-sour, perhaps chicken guy ding, and some beef ribs and penne with Italian sausage. I even took some of those green leafy things occasionally. Okay, so my tastes in food were a little weird at that time.

I am sure you have eaten at a buffet restaurant at some time in your life. When you sit down at your table and look at your plate piled high with food, you drink in the array of goodies just waiting to be devoured, salads, marinated vegetables, fish, chicken, pork or beef, and some starches or bread. Let's not forget those tantalizing side dishes. You have a wide variety of delectable items for your enjoyment. It is a menagerie of colour and delight. As you begin to eat, you start with your favourite. If your palate was adventuresome and experimental that evening, you might start eating by trying the new dish that smells the most inviting. You then move on to the next delightful morsel and enjoy its spicy fare. You move back and forth between the delicacies, enjoying the differences that each has to offer. Or are you the type that eats one dish completely, savouring all it has to offer your taste buds before moving on to the next adventure of culinary pleasure? Whatever your approach to enjoying this buffet, each food preparation is different, yet taken together, the combination of flavours, aromas, and textures orchestrates a wonderful and delicious meal. Oh yes, don't forget the sweet section; they don't want to be left out of the party. Who could have thought such a wide variety of dishes could provide such an enjoyable and nutritious meal!

During my meditation of October 23, 2012, I had an impression that life is really like that buffet. The variety of food represents the variety of psychological theories, philosophies, and even religions that are at our disposable for guidance, consideration, and adoption in our lives. If we are religious, we often settle on the one attended by our parents or the dominant religion of our culture. We may subscribe to some major psychology theory for life guidance, such as Abraham Maslow's hierarchy of needs. Perhaps we have adopted a philosophy of life based upon environmental values and the joys of nature. If we ignore or reject other disciplines, even within the overall context of our chosen philosophy, it is like going to a buffet and only eating potatoes, leaving everything else behind. Life can be enriched by sampling many dishes. Life can be more rewarding by examining and discovering other people's ideas and concepts concerning your chosen path in life.

For example, I was raised in the United Church under the Christian umbrella. During my teenage years, I attended half a dozen other denominations under that umbrella. Each one was interesting; however, I eventually decided that formal, organized religion was not for me.

When I learned to meditate, the first method I was taught was a step method, which meant visualizing colours and staircases. It was a visual process. It was effective in slowing the mind and allowing contact with the Divine Energy. I decided to venture further into the buffet of meditation and tasted different types of meditations. I wanted to have more experiences involving the Cosmic Energy. I learned a meditation technique involving the use of mantras that employ repetition of a sound either silently or openly. I learned energy meditation where mental concentration is focused on various areas of the body. Every technique brought forth a similar contact with Spirit. The meditation method I use today is a combination of what I have learned.

In my journey of sampling Cosmic Sacred Energy, mentioned previously, I learned how to give clairvoyant readings. I participated in lying-on-of-hands and therapeutic touch. I also studied life patterns and life cycles as revealed through western astrology. I enjoyed exploring shamanism, auras and spirit guides. Again, I was sampling more tasty dishes at the buffet of Spirit.

There's nothing wrong with staying with one philosophy in life if it gives you comfort, meaning, and connection to Divine Creation. However, my meditation that morning pointed out that there is much to be gained by exploring other related disciplines of the Spirit. Putting together your dinner of spiritual nourishment can be most rewarding by exploring the wisdom from many disciplines, not just your own group. Each discipline offers something exciting and stimulating for your spiritual health and growth and awaits your discovery. Just like those tasty morsels of food at the buffet that are waiting to awaken the taste buds on your tongue, each spiritual path awaits your discovery of the truths it has to offer. These truths will excite your soul, just like a buffet excites your appetite.

Although I cannot authenticate the following quote, it is a wonderful metaphor for life. It was related to me by an environmental photographer who has spent much time in Tibet and is very knowledgeable about Tibetan traditions. He mentioned during a conversation in early May 2013 at the Moab Photography Symposium in Moab Utah that the Dalai Lama said, "Spirit is the water. Religions are the tea and coffee we make with the water." Even if the Dalai Lama did not say this, I like this analogy. Let's take the time to taste each other's tea and coffee. Is the brew sweet, does it have a hint of hickory, or does it have a "wake you up" bitterness? Does it stand well on its own? Does it go well with mint or honey? How it is different from your own tea or coffee? We need to understand that our tea and coffee may taste different, but the source used to create it, water, is the same.

If you have embraced the religious traditions of your culture, why not experience parallel denominations? If you are a member of an Anglican church, try attending a Pentecostal service one Sunday or a Catholic service. Or go outside your umbrella and visit a Buddhist or Hindu temple. If your joy comes from transcendental meditative practices, why not experience a Chopra Centre meditation challenge? If you are a committed humanist, why not examine a different theory of psychology? Or go way overboard and investigate Western astrology as a personality theory! How about looking into numerology, tarot cards, or runes? I am referring to any philosophical practice here that does not promote harm to our fellow man. You will find beauty and knowledge in all these disciplines, and with an open mind, the information gained will expand your perspective and appreciation of Creation.

When you sample the many items at the buffet of spiritual knowledge, you come to realize that all dishes are tasty, valid, and good. Each one is a truth in is own right. When you venture out into other fields of human experience, your life becomes a greater source of gratification and happiness. You will see the good in all, which is a reflection of our Divine Nature.

It's Not Always About Me

We all live our lives the best way we know how. We respond to issues as they arise and make the appropriate decisions. Some of us have mentors in life from which we seek advice, people such as parents, siblings, or those in authority. Some of us are inspired by people who lived exceptional lives like Mahatma Gandhi or Mother Teresa. For the most part, our considerations are for the well-being of ourselves and our families and perhaps a few close friends. We give little consideration to strangers on a personal level. Occasionally, we may donate to the food bank or other charities. This may make us feel good and it is certainly an honourable activity, but unless you actually work or volunteer at the food bank, you do not emotionally interact with the people who benefit from your gift.

This book is about coming to the realization that we live in two worlds at the same time: the world of our physical senses and the realm of Spirit. I have shared how Spirit communicates to us and gives us direction through our night-time dreams, meditations, contemplations, intuitive feelings and especially coincidences. When I reflect back on my life, both overall and specific projects, I get chills and tingles of excitement when I see the action of Spirit weaving into my life, guiding me along, and helping me realize my dreams and goals.

One particular coincidence really stands out. I worked for a time in the retail music industry. Eventually I wanted to move to the wholesale side. The company I worked for had no opportunities so I decided to apply for work at a large diversified musical instrument manufacturer. I contacted the company and was given the name of the gentleman I needed to connect with. I will call him John. He was a busy man and I had a great deal of difficulty finding him in his office on my days off. Every time I made inquiries, he was out of town. I lived in Toronto where there are many winter storms. They can be fairly short-lived, but the snow makes the roads very treacherous and at times the wind reduces visibility to nearly zero. I was driving one winter afternoon when one of these storms blew up. Suddenly the roads became very slippery. I decided to pull over and ride the storm out at a large hotel. I knew that the hotel had an adequate lounge, just in case many other drivers had the same idea. I drove slowly into the parking lot and parked my car in the middle of this blinding blizzard. Another car pulled up beside me. We both got out of our vehicles at the same time and, bracing ourselves against the snow and wind, walked very briskly to the hotel. When we got to the lobby, for some unknown reason I introduced myself to this stranger. He then introduced himself to me: it was John from the music company I had been trying to contact for several weeks! We spent our time riding out the storm, discussing the wholesale music business.

However, life is not always about me. We live in this world with 7 billion other people to whom Creation is also offering guidance. There are times when we are other people's coincidences, especially when events in our lives do not go as planned or as you would have liked them to unfold. I will share with you three specific examples.

My wife and I enjoy our motorhome. We like the slow pace and flexibility this type of travel offers. Since we are retired, we often travel during the off season when things are less busy. We rarely make reservations for recreational vehicle parks. During one afternoon on a recent trip, much to our surprise, every park we stopped at was either full or didn't have the site size or amenities we needed. After three or four attempts, we finally found a park that had an opening and we set up our motorhome. Soon a family pulled into the site beside us. It became apparent they were having difficulties with the water hook-up. I carry a few extra accessories with me and had an adapter that could handle two water hoses from one connection. I offered my assistance. It turned out the water connection was fine. The problem was that they had left their pressure-reducing valve behind when they left the park from the previous night. The water pressure at most parks is far too high for direct connection to your motorhome or trailer. It will damage your plumbing unless you have a pressure-reducing valve. I had a spare valve. I lent it to them and they left it on our utility box the next morning when they left. This was neither a life-saving situation nor anything dramatic, but let's review what happened. We could not find a site that afternoon. Our efforts seemed to be blocked. We eventually found one after many attempts. A total stranger pulled up beside us in need of something that we had. This was a coincidence: two strangers travelling and coming together, revealing an unplanned opportunity to show some concern and respond to the needs of another.

I enjoy attending astrology conferences. I attended one in Seattle in May 2009. The lunch break on the second day found the restaurant in the hotel very busy. As I waited in line, I got involved in idle conversation with the lady next to me. When we reached the front of the line, there was only one table available, so we sat together. I must point out that I'm usually a bit of a recluse at times when I go to these conferences. I like to take a break from the subject matter. I like to recharge my mental batteries. Meal breaks are always part of my recharge time. Since we were both hungry, I passed up my routine and agreed to share the last table with this person. I soon learned that she had a consulting practice in California. We quickly established some common ground as she and her husband were in the final stages of a major home renovation, something my wife and I had done 10 years earlier. As is often the case with conversation between strangers, the talk turned to children. She asked me how many children I had. I told her my wife and I didn't feel compelled to raise a family, although our business certainly seemed like a demanding child at times. She asked why we made that decision. I explained the best I could why we chose that path. I pointed out that life can be very rewarding even without children. It is not a requirement for fulfilment and satisfaction in living. After my comments, she was quiet for a few moments and then said, "It is a no wonder I'm having lunch with you." It turned out she had been grappling with this issue of children for a long time, feeling motherhood was not for her. I guessed by her approximate age that she was putting pressure on herself or others were pressuring her to raise a family. She was feeling confused and extremely guilty about not wanting to enter the world of parenting. When we finished our lunch, she thanked me for sharing my stories. She said she felt very much at peace with herself and her decision regarding children. I never saw her again.

This is another example of Spirit arranging a conversation between two strangers. A story needed to be heard. I was part of her coincidence that afternoon.

As I mentioned earlier, I worked in the retail music business for a while. I sold pianos and electronic organs. Very early during that job, I was having problems making sales. One morning, I awoke with a very simple non-threatening idea for a sales closing technique. Whenever we had a potential customer look at an instrument, we would give them an order form to take home that recorded the model number and price. We would have the customer sit down at our sales desk as we prepared the form. This was provided so when they did decide to make a purchase, they would have the information needed. A secondary reason for this was since we all worked on commission, this would help track which salesperson had served the customer and thus receive the commission. My idea was to simply place the order form on the desk in front of the customer, place a pen beside it, and ask if they wanted to make a decision to buy right away. If they did, I would pay the sales tax (as sales people, we had some leeway with the selling price). When I arrived at the store that morning, which was in a large shopping mall, I decided to try this method with the first person who walked into the shop.

An elderly couple walked in shortly after I opened up for business, casually looking at a small electronic organ. They were really just in the mall for seniors' day. However, I had resolved to try my new technique with the very first person to enter the store. I thought to myself, "It probably won't work anyway. The technique is too simple." After the couple satisfied their curiosity and were about to leave the store, I tried my new method. To my utter astonishment, it worked! They bought the organ and we delivered it to their home the next day. Then I started to feel very remorseful. Yes, I needed the income, but why didn't I let that elderly couple leave the store and wait for the next person who showed interest in an instrument? They had to finance their purchase. I began to wonder what they would have to give up to make the payments on the bank loan. Hopefully not food!

A week passed and I was still feeling very badly for what I felt I had imposed on those elderly people. One morning while demonstrating a piano to a potential customer, I noticed every few minutes that an older gentleman would walk by the store. When my customer left, this older gentleman approached. It was the elderly man who had bought the organ the week before. I was about to apologize profusely when he put out his hand and shook mine. He said, "Thank you for selling us that organ. Whenever my wife's arthritis flares up, she sits down and plays and the pain disappears." He smiled and left.

This is another example of Spirit arranging results. I needed to learn a new sales technique, someone needed pain relief, and we met. Another coincidence.

I have had other situations where seemingly random events somehow become connected. We had a neighbour in the human resources consulting business that had a client who needed some marketing advice. She asked if I might help with this client as he had special needs. I was more than willing to help out. It turned out her client was an acquaintance from my university days.

I've had many instances where people have thanked me for my participation in something involving their lives. Something that was totally unexpected on my part. I'm sure many seemingly casual contacts with strangers in public places such as airplanes, lounges, or parties has led to people being motivated to follow a certain direction in their lives. I've often heard casual quotes at meetings that struck a chord with me and motivated me to start a particular project or continue with one I put on the shelf. We are often not aware how our words and actions will affect people. These situations are arrangements of Spirit.

We all live in this huge, alive, and breathing Universe, orchestrated and directed by an all-knowing Divine Intelligence. We have our lessons to learn, yet many times we unknowingly become involved with other peoples lives. We are other people's realizations, we are other people's answers to their questions, and we are other people's signposts for their lives. We are other people's coincidences.

It's not always about me!

PART IV
INNER VISION

That Quiet Place

Where did you spend your last vacation? Maybe you went to Rome. You took in the ancient ruins of the forum and coliseum. You imagined the crowds watching the entertainment of the day and wondered what it was like. You walked from the Trevi fountain to the Piazza Navona. You found your own favourite Rome piazza and sat for hours watching people walk by as you sipped espresso. You dined in one of the open-air restaurants that overlook the Pantheon. You dodged cars, motorcycles, and taxis everywhere. It was a very busy and chaotic city, but somehow relaxing, as it was a different environment than home.

Perhaps you vacationed at Seven Mile Beach on Grand Cayman Island in the Caribbean. You relaxed on the sand, stretched out in the sun, and swam in the refreshing water. You took a boat out to the reef and did some scuba diving and snorkelling. You saw the many neon colours of tropical fish. You almost put your hand on the spines of a sea urchin. The dive master stopped you at the last minute. You saw sting rays and sea turtles. It was a marvellous, rejuvenating holiday.

Maybe you spent a week reading your John Grisham novels sitting in your local park, enjoying the fresh air, gentle breezes, and the smell of summer flowers. You sipped your favourite latte. It was the only company you needed for a week. It was the perfect get-away vacation.

Wherever you took your holiday, the change of pace created a sense of calm and tranquillity within yourself. You felt relaxed and at ease. It was wonderful!

Then the holiday was over and your old routine took over.

Where did Rome, Seven Mile Beach, and your local park go? Well, they are still there; it is you who changed location and shifted your awareness.

When you meditate, relax, or just allow yourself to be still beside a gentle, flowing stream, you feel very peaceful. When you leave your meditation or that peaceful spot in nature and return to your busy and sometimes chaotic routine, that inner sense of peace and contentment is still there. When you smile at a stranger or express your concern for others by giving to the local food bank at Christmas time, that sense of connectedness was there before you smiled or made that donation. That quiet place will be waiting for you the next time you journey to your spirit side. It does not go away just because you are not making an immediate, conscious connection.

When we respond to life from our ego side, our spirit side does not disappear. It waits for us to return. Just like the place where we spent our vacation, it is still there; it is we who leave, and we can choose to return at any time. If we put off meditating, avoid giving out smiles, or decline to donate our resources to charities or volunteer our time, our spirit side will wait. It is still there, even though we are not acknowledging it at that moment.

To get to Rome or any vacation spot, we have to take a plane, train, or automobile. That takes time! We can contact this peaceful aspect of ourselves in an instant, at any moment we choose, through our attitudes. We can visit that quiet place within ourselves immediately, anytime, anywhere. It happens the moment we decide to go there; it is always present and it never goes away. It is part of our existence. It is our higher self.

Going to the Movies (A Love Story)

How have I learned to love?
What wisdom have I gained?
Knowledge practiced becomes wisdom.

The first two questions, from the Edgar Cayce material, are part of the life review our soul experiences shortly after death. The last statement is from the material presented by Doctor Brian Weiss in his book Many Lives, Many Masters. [62]

Two questions and a statement—sounds like a movie!

How does one learn to love? How does one gain wisdom?

Love is an overused word in Western culture with many different connotations and meanings. Can you love your car or favourite sports team the same as your spouse and family? I love chocolate and sunny days. Wine and cheese are another of my loves. My wife loves snow in the winter so she can ski. She loved her cats.

From the perspective of a life review, I believe love refers to how we have learned to help our fellow man by putting our own desires into context and perspective. Our desires drive us; they give us the will to get up in the morning. Without goals and desires, we would not be alive. Without direction, life can lose meaning. However, we need to examine where these wishes and desires lead us in life. Were your desires used for the betterment of the people and environment in which you lived? Or were they used strictly for self-gratification and self-entertainment? When we accomplish our goals in life others are also affected. We may not be aware of this because we were so focused on what we were doing. It is not just we who benefit from our accomplishments. If you decide to celebrate your achievements by having a gathering of friends at a local business establishment, the owner of the restaurant or lounge you frequent will benefit financially from your celebration. If you build your dream home, the tradesmen doing the building will gain employment. The suppliers of the building materials will benefit and be able to provide jobs for people who deliver those materials to your building site. If you finally get up the courage to take art lessons, the school will benefit from your attendance by receiving your tuition so they can pay the overhead for the school. If we decide to be less judgemental of others, people will probably find us more pleasant to be with. Whether we are cognizant of the fact or not, our actions and decisions affect others. When we decide to pursue our goals and desires, we generate a chain reaction where many people, often unknown to us personally, gain and benefit.

For example, one of my desires when I was a young man was to be millionaire. I hated paying rent; I felt it was money wasted. I bought a house as soon as I could. Then I needed furniture. A friend was in the process of separating from his wife. She had to sell some furniture. I bought it. The chain reaction was starting.

Home ownership was very important to me as I felt it was a component of wealth. When my wife wanted to start her business, I didn't think twice about selling our house to raise the money necessary. Even though this went against my earlier decisions about not paying rent, the business opportunity held potential for generating wealth. It fit with my plans as well. When we rented a house, our landlord benefited as he was trying out a new job in another province and wanted a relatively short-term tenant to watch his place until he decided to sell the house. When the landlord wanted to sell, the business was at a point where it could return our start-up cash and we built a new home. Again, the chain reaction set in.

If my motivation for wealth was to feel superior to others and to be able to enjoy the best material goods and lifestyle so others would be envious, then this is not learning how to love or gain wisdom. I must admit, I purchased a certain vehicle when my best friend said he would be extremely jealous if I ever owned such a vehicle. I obviously had a lot to learn!

If my motivation to gather wealth was to hire people so they could achieve their desires such as paying off their mortgage or saving the money necessary for school or a vacation, then my desires would be more in line with "love". If I wanted wealth to support a new local restaurant or business and help them achieve their goals and dreams, then I have learned how to "love". If I increased my charity donations as my income increased, then I was learning how to "love".

When we see that our dreams, goals, and desires have an effect on the people and environment around us, then we begin to perceive our interconnectedness on a non-material spiritual plane. When we perceive and realize we can make a small difference to someone else's life by pursuing our own desires, then we become more aligned with our divine nature. We become more thoughtful and sympathetic as this awareness expands within our being. Our environment begins to reflect this back to us as more gentle and caring people appear in our lives.

It is from this attitude and mindset that wisdom appears. The more we realize our spiritual connection to each other and use this knowledge as a consideration for our actions, the wiser we become in our motivation and decision-making.

Knowledge practised becomes wisdom!

The Holiday

My wife and I are planning a summer trip to Oregon. She's been pouring over maps, RV campsite directories, photography websites, and everything to find the best spots to photograph in Oregon. She's adding up the mileage and stops based upon the types of roads, estimating the time it will take to reach our next destination. She asks my opinion on locations and distances and then makes changes. There is a constant readjustment of the plans as bookings for RV sites do not fit like a glove. New maps are purchased, photography gear checked, and passports verified. The motorhome is serviced, and arrangements are made for someone to watch the house when we are gone. Bills coming due while away are paid in advance. All this preparation for just a three-week trip!

Perhaps a holiday is a metaphor for life itself. Do we plan our lives before we are born? Do we decide the experiences we want to undergo? Do we choose our parents, family, and culture so we will get the best life available to fit our plans? In her book Sacred Contracts, Caroline Myss discusses this possibility in a convincing manner. [63]

When I read her book, it reminded me of a holiday. Like our trip to Oregon, you the reader may also do some planning for future travel, perhaps to Europe. You research your trip and what opportunities will be there for your enjoyment. You make accommodation arrangements and consult travel guides for restaurants and tours. You decide walking tours of the streets of Paris will give you a feel for the city, allowing for spontaneous decisions. Decisions like deciding what bistro to stop at for lunch or coffee. What museum or art gallery looks interesting? You do not have the option to make spontaneous decisions in your home environment. Everything is always very structured and follows routines. Making on the spot, spontaneous decisions sounds like fun!

Your appreciation of music takes you to the Opera not only in Paris but also in Budapest. Your interest in engineering draws you to the canals of Amsterdam. Your love of fresh air and nature makes the Swiss Alps a must-see. Your deep interest in history puts the Stonehenge in England on your list. Everything you plan reflects your personal interests and what you wish to discover, both familiar and not so familiar. It is almost like a different lifetime!

Then it is time to return home. The guidebooks are left behind. You gather your thoughts and experiences together, perhaps write a journal, or make some notes to guard against the inevitable fading of your memory as time passes.

You fly back home. Your friend picks you up at the airport. Immediately, you are asked questions. What was it like? Did you get to do everything you wanted? Would you go back there again? You explain how exciting it was to see Notre Dame Cathedral and the Opera House in Paris. That quaint bistro two blocks from your hotel where you watched the Parisians start their day with croissants and café au lait. You became adept at making on the spot decisions. It was very rewarding. The opera you heard in Budapest was very moving and inspiring. As a result, you bought a violin there and will start taking lessons as soon as you find a teacher. Your holiday transformed you into the person you wanted to be: a decision maker, taking music lessons rather than just listening. You became involved with your life to a greater extent and feel more alive. It was marvellous!

Perhaps as Edgar Cayce suggests, upon death, our immortal soul is asked some questions as it reviews the life just left behind. How did I learn to love? What wisdom did I gain? Perhaps we'll look at our lives from the perspective of what our soul wished to experience before it was born. Perhaps love and wisdom were some of the yardsticks our spirit wished to engage in while in human form. Perhaps these are some of the gauges for success and enjoyment in life.

Perhaps life really is a holiday!

Forgiveness

When I was 25 years old, I lost my job, fired less than six months after I was hired. I had found the job through a placement agency that put a six-month guarantee on me; apparently, I didn't live up to the expectations of my employer. This surprised me. It was my first job in that field and after basic training I was told to visit the customers in my territory and get to know them. They would in turn get to know me. "Don't worry about the sales," I was told. There will be major training at head office in a few months.

Five and a half months passed and I got the call—you're fired. No explanations. "Leave the keys to the company car on the desk," I was told.

Up to that time, I took pride in my ability to get along with people, even difficult people. Being fired for no specific or apparent reason stunned me. I felt like an arrow had been shot through my heart. It was very painful emotionally.

I searched through my memories of the past six months. I could see where I could have shown more initiative in learning the product line rather than following my employers' direction of not worrying about sales. There was a day spent with the product specialist that was very rocky. But neither of these issues was raised. I was just shown the door.

We often encounter situations in our relationships with people that do not produce the result we wanted. Sometimes the response of others to things we have done is very inappropriate and harmful. Sometimes we are accused of doing or not doing something and the accuser will not consider their contribution to the dilemma. Oftentimes this leads to a complete lack of communication and a blurring of the facts. The opportunity for clarification disappears, yet life must go on.

These types of situations can start an endless search to answer the question "Why?" In the case of my being fired without any given reasons, my mental state became cloudy and confused. We all have these endless searches in our lives. They can be triggered by many instances from daily life. Why did my friend explode that evening and leave my life forever? Why did my teacher fail me when I know I aced the exam? Why did my teenage son ransack the local city park and do so much damage? Why did I behave in such an inappropriate manner at the reception? Yes, our endless whys do not necessarily originate from other people's actions; sometimes our own actions can be just as mysterious.

Now we come to our choices. Do we continue the endless mental searches? Do we hold on to the stress and frustration being generated by our mental worries? Do we seek revenge anyway, not knowing why? Do we deny it happened and live in denial? Or do we consider something else like forgiveness, including of ourselves?

Forgiveness is not a process of planned and carefully thought-out forgetfulness. It is awareness that our lives are more than just one moment. Our lives are an accumulation of many experiences, both in this incarnation and in past lives. We can spend our energies focusing on the wounds of life or call upon our higher selves and express those divine qualities. Forgiveness opens the door to our sacred selves and allows personal happiness and harmony to flow into our lives and those around us. Yes, this is much easier said than done, especially in cases where extreme abuse has occurred.

In the words of Mark Twain, "Forgiveness is the fragrance that the violet sheds on the heel that just crushed it." [64] According to the Mayo Clinic, "Forgiveness is a decision to let go of resentment and thoughts of revenge. Forgiveness can lead to feelings of understanding, empathy, and compassion for the one who hurt you." [65] These are the divine qualities within your being, accessed and generated by your decision. Edward T.

Creagan M.D. says "Forgiveness is a gift you give yourself." [66]

When forgiveness enters your consciousness, you cease to define your life by the hurts from daily life. You are free to live your life from your own perspective and desires. You have the freedom to use your energy for the creative expression of your own divine nature. You are free to be yourself. This is your gift to yourself.

Say yes to freedom!

Scepticism

I made two big assumptions, based upon my personal experiences, in writing this book. These assumptions are we are all part of an immense Divine Creation and we are learning our role in its scheme. This Creation is loving in nature. It rejoices in our steps of understanding as we live and grow individually and collectively as a species. We do this ourselves; no Messiah deity or anyone else can do it for us.

Some of you may be highly sceptical of this opinion regarding our existence. After all, no one in my church or the universities I attended mentioned anything like this. You may believe everything that is real can be measured and accounted for, and everything else lives only in fantasy and imagination, as idle minds fabricate myths about our existence. You may also believe if such a force existed, we would have known it by now. After all, mankind has inhabited the earth for over three thousand years.

Let's take an imaginary journey. Imagine a grade three school class. The teacher has given all the students a test in basic mathematics. The results have been handed out and the teacher leaves. The school session is over and no one knows if or when the teacher may return, next year or next millennium.

The class has a dilemma. Some students understand the concept of mathematics better than others and they enjoy the subject. Some have very little understanding and dislike the subject immensely, but still feel part of the class. Their collective challenge is whether they continue studying mathematics as a group. The ones with the most understanding would act as teachers. Or do they let the entire topic disappear?

The students who didn't pass the test and disliked mathematics want to forget it. They become very vocal and eventually create anti-mathematics movements to hide their ignorance. They form great organizations to denounce mathematics as a valid field of study. They generate falsehoods and outright lies about the subject in an attempt to influence those in grades one and two to stay away from the subject when they reach grade three.

The brightest ones know the folly of confrontation and form their own secret mathematics club and flourish in their understanding. They study deep into the theories of the subject. They are overjoyed with their discoveries and the new knowledge their studying is revealing to them.

The members of the anti-mathematics movement see the cheerfulness on the faces of the mathematicians and become very jealous. They start to wonder why they are so happy. Because they cannot understand why they are smiling so much, they start to fear the mathematicians. They eventually declare war on them and go about a systematic destruction of all libraries and places were the knowledge of mathematics exists.

The mathematicians go further underground and continue to thrive.

Many generations pass and they are now starting to surface, talking about the wondrous topic of mathematics. The few who listen are very sceptical. This is all crazy thinking. How can you calculate a rocket's route to the moon? I don't think so! Rockets will not fly that far. They fall to earth after a few hundred meters. It has never been done! But the mathematicians have been studying. They have discovered the relationship between the center of gravity and the center of pressure that is required for stable rocket flight. [67] Many watch the rocket reach the moon! Then they ask, where was this science hidden for all these years? Once a truth has been shown, the believers appear. It becomes accepted fact.

When scepticism clouds our thinking, we are like the grade three students who dislike mathematics. Often scepticism is just ignorance (due to lack of study only, nothing biological) and fear raising its head.

We need to realize that our understanding of our true divine nature, individually and collectively, is a lot like those grade three students. Our established institutions of learning have not embraced the concept of a spiritual force available to all for guidance, protection, and peaceful living. There is much evidence that proves such energy exists. The best book I have read concerning this is The Field by Lynne McTaggart. [68] It is an amazing collection of scientific experiments that support the existence of a divine force within us, written in a manner that all can comprehend.

We have a ways to go before our graduation day appears. However, with a conscious application of our intelligence and the development of our perceptions, our graduation will eventually arrive. Our scepticism will evaporate. We will know we are part of this beautiful Divine Creation and that each of us has personal access to it through our attitudes and decisions. With this realization, we will be truly enlightened!

Deception

During the summer of 1984, there was a national election in Canada. During the televised debate on July 25, the liberal Prime Minister, Mr. John Turner, was questioned by his rival, Mr. Brian Mulroney, the leader of the conservative party. Canadians were growing very weary of the time-honoured political process of patronage–basically political appointments to high paying jobs as a reward for service to the party. Mr. Turner had just overseen over 200 such appointments as a favour to the outgoing leader of his party, Mr. Pierre Trudeau. During the debate, Mr. Mulroney, sensing the mood of the country, raised his arm with an accusing finger pointed directly at Mr. Turner and said, "You had an option to say no." He demanded Mr. Turner apologize to Canadians for not cancelling the appointments. He implied that if elected, no such things would happen under a conservative government. Mr. Mulroney and his conservative party went on to win the election, a landslide record-setting win with the biggest election majority in Canadian history. [69]

Was he truthful or did he use deception? David J. Mitchell, in his article Patronage Nation from the Ottawa Citizen on June 27, 2009, wrote "the Mulroney administration proved to be just as focused and efficient in distributing appointments and rewards to friends and supporters as any government of the modern era." [70] So much for truth! Political promises made during election campaigns in all countries are certainly viewed with a high degree of disbelief. Deception to gain votes is nothing new in the political field; it certainly worked in Canada in 1984.

Many years ago, I purchased twelve-grain bread, thinking it was the healthiest bread available at the time. After using this product for about two years, I read the ingredients' label. Imagine my surprise to find the first ingredient was enriched white flour—not what I was expecting. I felt deceived. I recently read the ingredients label on a bottle of pomegranate juice: it was mainly grape juice with flavouring. More deception.

After my second year of university, I was hired by a local conservation authority to work in a local park. They hired several university students that year. When we got our first pay check, the hourly rate was 10 per cent less than what we were promised during our interviews. We approached the park superintendent and asked about this discrepancy. He laughed and said we were wrong and that he never said we would earn more than the rate indicated on the pay stubs. We had been purposely deceived, it appeared. During my years working as a sales representative, many bonus schemes were presented during job interviews that never lived up to their promise. Some jobs were completely misrepresented. I accepted a job as a creative advertising consultant for a publishing firm. I discovered after I reported to work that they only wanted me to sell advertising space in their magazines.

Recently, a friend received a persistent phone call after taking a survey. Her daughter took the call one day and suggested that she should contact them. She seemed to think the call was genuine and that she had won a prize of some sort. With some hesitation, my friend called and yes, she had won a travel voucher. The company would like to deliver it personally to her door, saying it would only take five minutes. After being assured by the person on the phone that it would be no longer than five minutes and no product demonstrations were involved, she finally agreed to give them her home address. At the appointed time, a vacuum cleaner salesman showed up at her door and wouldn't leave. He wasted two hours of her time before he gave her the travel voucher. She threw it in the garbage, disgusted with the deception and outright lies the company used to try and sell their product, not to mention the waste of her time.

We see deception almost everywhere. There are laws against

fraud and false advertising, yet half-truths and deception persist everywhere from food labelling, product selling, and political campaigning. Why is deception so rampant in our society?

Why do politicians seem to think they need to deceive to win elections?

Why do some manufacturers think they need to mislead their customers to sell their product?

Why do some employers stretch the truth about the position they are filling?

Deception is a result of a lack of understanding of our true selves. It is an expression of a deep-felt feeling of powerlessness, a sense that we have little influence on our lives. There is a lack of contact with the creative force within.

We are the co-creators of our lives, environments, and societies. The Cayce readings talk about this relationship with the divine. "The Cayce philosophy promises ... you are an extraordinary being with powers to shape your life ... each one of us ... has the opportunity to be a cocreator with God." [71] This is the basis of visualization: we decide what it is we wish to achieve, accomplish or change in our lives and we create the image in our minds, which presents it to the Universe. We then listen and watch for directions as to how to reach our goal. When we understand this co-creative relationship with the divine, deception is not necessary. It would be avoided at all costs because knowledge of spiritual law—as you sow, so shall you reap—will prevent deception.

When we discover how we have real power and influence over our own lives, we begin to live as we were designed by nature. As we use this awareness of our true selves and become cognizant of its presence, individually and collectively, the need for deception will disappear. It will be replaced with clarity of purpose and openness to all.

Accidents

We've all had accidents, those unplanned adventures that are always inconvenient. I believe accidents can be actually planned events, events you orchestrated prior to incarnating into this life. Let me explain.

Have you ever taken an afternoon nap or gone to your studio to paint, write, or create something? You decide on the amount of time you wish to spend doing the activity. However, you know you will get so absorbed in your project—especially if it is taking a cat nap—that you ask your spouse, roommate, colleague, or alarm clock to notify you when the time you allotted is up.

We live in two worlds: the world of our physical senses and the world of our spirit. We inhabit these planes simultaneously. Our senses can take over and have such a strong hold on our attention that our soul is often ignored or never acknowledged.

I believe we plan our lives like we plan a vacation. Our souls research our life experiences and establish a time frame for those lessons to be learned. Not unlike grade school where after several months, it is assumed each student will have learned enough to go on the next level. A lifespan can offer many themes and lessons from the extremes of self-sacrifice and total compassion like Mother Teresa to total self-absorption like a narcissistic movie star, rock musician, athlete, or politician. Other lifespan themes could be the need for self-assertion, addressing fears, the futility of violence, or the need for balance in all we do. These themes can change as we grow and mature over time. All experiences teach us something that brings us more into alignment with our true spiritual selves. For some, the realizations of our life's purposes are often discovered only after the body has been discarded by the soul (death).

We get so involved in our physical life and the information our physical senses present us, we ignore or cannot see our soul issues. We miss the patterns in our experiences that point to what we are trying to accomplish from a spiritual perspective. To compensate for this, prior to our births, we set alarm clocks or ask our celestial friends to wake us up as we travel through this holiday called life. Accidents are coincidences, perhaps last resort coincidences, from our friends, responding to our plans, doing what we asked of them, to keep us on our chosen soul path. Accidents are part of the human experience.

Five years after my experience near the Bay of Fundy, I was painting the exterior of a house. The extension ladder I was standing on collapsed and I fell two stories to the pavement below. I described this accident in the chapter "The Challenges" under "Attitudes Towards Healing." I will reiterate the story here again with more details. I shattered my right ankle, my leg bone protruding through the skin. It took the surgeon over two hours to reset my ankle. It took three and a half weeks for the swelling to go down enough so a cast could be fitted on the ankle. This was in the days of plaster casts, so every four to six weeks, I would return to the hospital. Each time the old cast was removed, my ankle was x-rayed to monitor the healing process and a new cast was put on. The surgeon would show me the x-rays each time. He was watching for a membrane over the bone to form so the bone would heal. After nine months, the upper part of the ankle showed no signs of healing and the membrane was not growing. Needless to say, I was very frustrated and willing to try anything. My older sister had a friend who was involved in a spiritual healing group. I met with her. We discussed premonitions, dreams, and other activities of the spirit. She said her healing group would work on me and she gave me an exercise to do. I was to visualize my ankle being whole and the membrane forming, as I was falling off to sleep. I did this every night. Within a week, I could feel the bottom of my foot for the first time in nine months. It had been numb all that time. Three weeks later when I had my ankle x-rayed, the membrane was present and the upper part of my ankle under that membrane was completely healed! When I started walking again, the ankle was extremely painful. The accident was so severe that the lower bones in the ankle were very much out of alignment and had to be fused together. I eventually had to get a bone graft from my hip to fuse the lower joint of my ankle (This is a wonderful example of how a combination of spirit and physical manipulation in healing can bring results).

How can an accident like this be a planned event? As I mentioned in the chapter entitled The Challenges under Problems With Psychic Abilities, after my experience by the Bay of Fundy, one of the immediate issues for me was accepting the psychic ability of premonitions. When I shattered my ankle, I was still trying to ignore these psychic happenings. I actually asked them to leave me alone and go away. They didn't listen. They hung around. I couldn't understand what was happening and I was not making any effort to investigate or study the phenomenon. I would talk about it with a few people from time to time; however, most thought I was somewhat crazy. My accidental fall forced my attention back into spiritual activity and led me to spiritual healing. Premonitions and the sense of déjà vu are interesting; however, I now saw that spirit also has a healing capacity well beyond the grasp of reason and the intellect.

It forced me to delve deeper into the spiritual side of life that I had been having problems accepting and understanding. It showed me a different aspect of my spirit that I would never have imagined: the ability to contribute to the healing process. I experienced first hand the role visualization plays in this process. The concept of a goal, a healed ankle, and how it is achieved was baffling for its apparent simplicity.

I shared this experience with very few people. It was quite unbelievable—only a lunatic would believe such a thing. When my wife's business partner, Ralph, was gravely ill with an inoperable tumour in his brain stem, I decided to share this story with him. He was hospitalized and could not speak. He was not a very open-minded person to anything non-traditional. I had no idea how he might respond to the story. He died about three weeks later. Shortly after his death, our two cats would not walk through the entrance foyer of our home. They would slink along the walls and then make a mad dash into the basement. It was very unusual and a bit disconcerting. We asked some friends to meditate on our house. They said Ralph was there and wanted to communicate with us. We meditated, and sure enough, both my wife and I received the same message from him. He told us to keep believing what we believe in and visualize the result you want. It is a Truth. The cats returned to normal. We never heard from Ralph again.

My ankle experience was a powerful wake-up call and propelled me on my journey towards a self-directed study of meditation and body-mind relationships. It gave a certainty and conviction that my existence involved the spiritual as well as the physical. My broken ankle got me on track as to what my soul wished to experience in this human sojourn. Knowledge and expression of the divine energy within seemed to be on the agenda. Ignoring it and asking this to go away did not appear to be in the cards! The accident was a signpost pointing towards the path I should be taking.

Two years later, I had an automobile accident. I had just started a job as a real estate agent and felt I needed a luxury car to appear successful. My search for a vehicle brought me to a navy blue, barely used, sleek and beautiful Ford Thunderbird. I was discussing this vehicle with my best friend and he stated he would be extremely jealous if I ever bought that car. When I heard how he felt about the vehicle, I decided to buy it to see his reaction. Can you imagine a more stupid reason to buy a vehicle than to provoke envy in another person? This is not an honourable path to walk. Certainly not the path a soul seeking divine expression would meander down.

Three months later, I had a minor accident with the car. Another driver drifted into my lane as I was turning right. He clipped my left fender, scraping the paint, denting the fender, and breaking the headlights. He was a World War II veteran returning home from his local Legion hall. He was very drunk. The police officer who attended the accident had to steady him as he walked over to the police car. When the report was filed, I went on my way.

An hour later, I was involved in another accident. This time, it was much more serious. I was hit broadside by a vehicle travelling at one hundred kilometres an hour. Not wearing a seat belt, I was thrown about inside the car, my glasses flying off my face. I ended up in the ditch beside the highway, with the hood bent up and the car hissing. I thought it was about to explode. I opened the door and staggered a few meters away and lay down in the summer grass. Soon, other people gathered around. The other driver and I were whisked away by ambulance to the local hospital. My navy blue, like new, sleek and beautiful Thunderbird was completely destroyed and so was the other car. The other driver died about five minutes after we arrived at the emergency room. As it turned out, he also was a World War II veteran who had spent the afternoon at his local Legion hall and was coincidentally a friend of a friend. He had been drinking heavily and had been offered a ride home but declined. That decision and my being in the wrong place at the wrong time cost him his life. What did this accident tell me?

Firstly, it sent a clear message that doing anything to provoke a negative response such as envy is not the path of a spiritually-minded individual. I am convinced that's why my Thunderbird was destroyed. My motivation was not honourable and did not align with divine principles like showing respect and restraint. This was the main lesson. I needed to work on expressing my divine self over my ego self. My focus needed to be on learning to walk the unseen spiritual path. My life compass had to be reset.

Secondly, a few years later while doing some past life regressions, I learned that I had lived in Italy during the Second World War. I was an Italian army Staff Sergeant, the last son of a career Italian general. My life ended when the building I was in was destroyed by an Allied forces bomb. Perhaps my tangle with two World War II veterans was karmic in nature. Perhaps this accident had a deeper meaning than just a life correction.

From the soul's perspective, life is a continuum. There is no birth and there is no death, only different bodies in different circumstances. Each lifespan has a goal, a purpose, and a lesson to be learned. Accidents are part of these lessons. Accidents are our celestial friends responding to us, just as we requested. They are the alarm clock we set to wake us at a given time. Accidents keep us on our chosen path or, in the case of fatal accidents, tell us our pleasant holiday is over and it's time to come home.

Body Memories

The Edgar Cayce readings make reference to Akashic records. These are also mentioned in Theosophy writings. Akashic records are the memories of each soul's journey over time registered in the Universe's super computer system. It is the central storehouse for the actions and thoughts of every individual who ever lived upon the earth.

Some believe accessing these records through prayer, guided meditation, or hypnosis can give greater insight into current life conditions. In his book Many Lives, Many Masters, Doctor Brian Weiss takes us through the healing journey of the first patient in his practice who, through hypnosis, accessed her Akashic records and relived her past lives. As she went through this process, her clinical symptoms of stress and neuroses diminished greatly. [72]

At a recent seminar I attended, put on by Doctor Weiss, he talked about a medical colleague who suffered severe back pain. His colleague could not find any relief for many years. Eventually he consulted Doctor Weiss and through hypnosis discovered he had been lanced in the back during a medieval battle and died. Upon this revelation, his back pain diminished. Do our soul's Akashic records carry body memories as well?

I was recently introduced to myofascial release massage. During my first treatment, a hip sore for a year and a knee sore for eight years felt much better. They seemed to be better aligned physically. They were still uncomfortable, but somehow operating more naturally and freely.

During the treatment, I would experience a dance of colours

before my closed eyes. These colours included blues, violets, purples, silver, and red–almost the entire spectrum. I often see colours in my consciousness while I meditate, and these colours were just as vivid and in some cases more vivid. I saw shades of blue I hadn't recalled seeing in many years.

My second treatment a month later started out with the continuation of the light show. About halfway through the session, I started sensing sources and causes of bodily pain and discomfort. I felt like a blacksmith's anvil had just crushed my right foot and ankle. Then my right hip felt like it was being burned by fire. My lungs felt like they were being scorched by fire as well. A little later, my left knee felt like it was being shattered while riding a horse in a scene of chaos and confusion, like a battlefield. While the therapist was working on my neck, a sense of drowning took over me. Was this my wild imagination? I'm not sure, but it felt like I was releasing body memories from past lives. It was neither frightening nor upsetting. On the contrary, it was rather liberating.

What I found interesting was that all the points of injury were areas of my body that were injured in my life–except for the drowning! Although I love being near the water and enjoy all types of boating, I have never been fond of being in the water and didn't learn to swim until I was 10 years old.

This experience suggests to me that not only do we carry our soul's experiences from past lives in our Akashic records, but we also carry memories of our past body experiences. As it is our innate divine nature to manifest and express who we are, it would seem logical that we have the potential to re-experience the bodily wounds from past lives to some degree. Although I suspect not every stubbed toe will be recreated, I suspect injuries associated with strong emotion would be more likely to linger as an imprint on our soul experience and be manifested in some related way through the body we have in this lifetime.

I look forward to more sessions of this type of massage, not just for the physical release and benefits. It may also lead to a better understanding of how we create circumstances in our lives that appear random and rooted in no apparent physical reason or cause.

I do not think this is just a passing observation. I believe we can learn something to help us in the here and now. The work of Dr. Weiss has shed light on how visiting past trauma can have positive effects on our lives today. Such understanding may help in the realization that choice is one of the most powerful tools we have in our lives. The people who chose to consult with Dr. Weiss were taking a step beyond their ego self and approaching their soul self, with the guidance of Dr. Weiss. They came away from these sessions with much relief from their discomforts, some physical, some emotional.

We can choose to remain ego-oriented or strive to be more soul-oriented. With caring and showing concern as our guide, both for ourselves and others, I believe we can influence the cycles that inhabit our consciousness from all lifetimes, including this one. This would lessen the impact they have on the body we currently inhabit.

By embracing the concept that our souls incarnate into this life with attitudes and experiences carried over from previous human lifetimes, we can lessen the discomforts of today's living. By attempting to understand our limitations and challenges from a soul perspective rather than exclusively from a bodily perspective, we can liberate ourselves from a great deal of unnecessary suffering. By consulting and following our spirit, we can live more carefree and comfortable lives. Body memories can become the friends that lead us to places of serenity and peace of mind.

Where Do All the Souls Come From?

As mentioned earlier, I recently attended a seminar presented by Dr. Brian Weiss. During the question-and-answer session, a participant pointed out that the global population is now seven billion and climbing. She then asked, where do all the souls come from?

Doctor Weiss's answer followed the opinions of others, mainly claiming that we humans are naïve to think that we on this earth are the only life in this massive universe. Just like high schools, of which there are hundreds spread around the country, we all go to the school of life in many different places.

For over 30 years, part of my monthly routine has been to have a therapeutic massage. During this time, I get so relaxed, I often hover at that level of consciousness we experience just before going off to sleep. Sometimes I do go to sleep! Although I cannot verify it, I seem to visit past lives or my imagination gets so stimulated I imagine some very bizarre stories. For instance, I once witnessed myself as a grown boy being offered to an Egyptian King's court by my family to be a member of the staff. I would be attending to the Pharaoh King himself. The one requirement was I could not recognize the King. How do you work in the Royal court and not look at the King? The court Doctor applies an instrument to your eyes and damages them. The damage does not create full blindness, but the sight is distorted enough so you cannot see the features of the King.

I was being prepared for this procedure. My family was very proud. We were being blessed and revered by all. My eyesight was destroyed.

Is this historically accurate? I have no idea. But I do not see how I could imagine such a bizarre scenario. I have seen myself as a young girl witnessing the death of her father. He was trampled to death by a fast moving army of horsemen riding past the front of our home. It seemed to be in early America. I have seen myself as a kidnapped woman in Northern Africa. It seemed like post-Egyptian times. I was involved in a ritual fertility ceremony. It was spring and the men were addressing the need for a fruitful harvest. I have seen myself as a boy on the eastern shore of the Mediterranean Sea. I was watching the approach of a Roman army. The quality of these imaginations is not like idle wakeful day dreaming about some fantasy. The quality is always very similar to the images I have seen while doing past life regressions. They have a vividness and organized nature to them. So my conclusion is that they are fragments of past lives revisited. Mostly during my massages, I experience a sense of peace and often perceive explosions of colour in front of my closed eyes. These occurrences are infrequent.

Recently, I had a very unusual incidence during my massage. I was in my usual pre-sleep state when I started dreaming. I cannot remember the contents, but I remember I was watching two very different dreams at the same time, like two movie screens side by side showing different movies. In my dreams, I am always involved and I was watching myself doing two different things simultaneously. Suddenly, my logic seemed to break through and said it is impossible to be having two dreams at the same time—you can only have one! They both disappeared.

I'm not a psychologist, but I can identify three parts of myself in this happening: the part that observes, the part that thinks, and the part that experiences (the dreamer). The experiencing part seems to be split into two, not pathologically like split personalities but both being active at exactly the same time.

In their book, Miracles and Other Realities, Lee Pulos and Gary Richman describe the life of a gifted Brazilian psychic named Thomaz. He was born in 1947 and was struck by lightning on his twelfth birthday. He separated from his body and while hovering above it and received a message about using a healing energy to help others before he was reunited with his body. He went on to display amazing psychic abilities in healing physical illness. He had other unexplainable talents. In one instance, he was able to take unfertilized chicken eggs and concentrate his energy on these eggs to produce live chicks in nine minutes! It is a very interesting book that reads like fiction, but it is not. All the stories were verified by many credible witnesses such as physicians and judges. One story describes how this man was physically seen in two different locations many miles apart, again verified by credible witnesses. [73] This concept is known as bilocation.

In his book, The Divine Matrix, Gregg Braden describes more verified stories of bilocation. One story is about Maria de Agreda, a Spanish Nun. From the 1620-1631, she reported over 500 journeys, where she would "fly" across the ocean to a distant land, even though she never left her convent. She would teach the people of this strange land the stories in the Bible. When the Spanish were on their exploration and conquest of Central America, a story emerged. They came across a village that was displaying Christian symbols. The natives told of how a woman would appear to them and teach them Biblical stories. The description was that of a European Nun. No nuns had been in that area of Central America!

Only after Maria de Agreda described the area's geography and climate to a church examination council were her mystical journeys declared authentic. She was given the consideration of "the highest rank among the mystics of past ages." [74]

There are many stories recorded about a Franciscan priest in southern Italy, Padre Pio, who lived from 1887 to 1968. He also had the ability to bilocate. During a prayer meeting in 1918 with a group of nuns, he apparently went to sleep. He could not be revived, even when shaken. When he did wake up and was later questioned about his behaviour, he stated he had been in America. During World War II, the pilots on a bombing raid over an Italian town saw a small priest in the sky in front of them and then all their bomb doors were jammed, preventing the destruction of that area. One of the pilots, when he later met Padre Pio, recognized him as the monk in the sky that night. [75]

Are these actual bilocations or a man using his spiritual nature beyond what most of us are aware? Whatever the truth is, these stories shed light on little-known and unused attributes of the spiritual side of human existence.

We observe in nature how the offspring of animals and plants have the same characteristics as the "parent." If we can accept that we are part of divine creation and have the ability to express divine attributes of this creation, such as kindness, cooperation, compassion and love, let's take this another step. Divine intelligence creates each of us as an offspring of itself. As offspring, we inherit and are capable of expressing the qualities of this Intelligence. We are all the same on a spiritual level. If divinity can divide itself into human droplets of itself, is it not too bizarre to think that we may also have this potential ability?

Perhaps our divine souls have the potential ability to divide and experience two different physical situations simultaneously. Experiencing the excesses of Western culture at the same time as experiencing the extremes of poverty in sub-Saharan Africa would certainly drive home the glaring economic imbalance in the world. This would help awaken sympathy and generosity towards our spiritual brothers and sisters. Perhaps some advanced souls can divide themselves just as our Divine Creator divides itself. Perhaps this is one of the sources of the seven billion plus souls inhabiting the earth. There may be many souls bilocating all around us right now. There may be very advanced souls who have chosen to arrive here and spend some time with us humans.

Perhaps at this time in our history, we are in need, as a race, of more advanced souls among us. They may be able to educate us or inspire us. Perhaps they will show us the futility of our ways, particularly the violence against each other. Perhaps with their help, we will discover the light of greater compassion within ourselves. I like visitors like that. We have room for them in our high school. Let's welcome them to our little blue planet.

Ego and Soul

Accepted psychological theory asserts we need a healthy ego to function in today's societies and cultures. What is a healthy ego? The word itself is Latin for "I" and in Freudian psychology, it is that part of our personalities that is responsible for dealing with reality. Too much ego can lead to narcissism—an inflated sense of self-importance.

Perhaps ego has another purpose. When we are children and developing our personalities, the ego starts to form as a result of feedback from our physical senses. It only sees things outside of us like trees, animals, planets, flowers, wind, rain, snow, thunder, and lightning. All these things are happening in our environment, including people such as our parents, siblings, relatives, and neighbours. Everything appears to be separate from ourselves, and physically it is. Some people hold our hands and others give us a pat on the back or a hug, but everything appears disconnected.

Eventually the sensory feedback we get is divided into two types: those situations giving us pleasant feelings or actions and those giving us unpleasant interactions. As time passes, the ego learns to stand on guard to prevent the unpleasant situations. It develops a strong need to be in control at all times, not unlike an overprotective parent standing on guard for their child. The ego starts to view the world as a threat. To protect itself, the ego learns to generate fear whenever it feels threatened or a loss of control. An attitude starts to seep into consciousness that says "Everything is separate from me and I need to be watchful and careful."

Ego will defend itself vigorously; it must be right at all costs. There is little sense of unity or community beyond family. If a sense of unity develops and expands to include culture and country, it is usually viewed as a collection of individual egos.

According to the Upanishads, the collection of philosophical texts that form the theoretical basis for the Hindu religion, there are two selves in us. They are compared to two birds who sit in a tree: one watches silently, the Seer or soul, while the other is engaged in various actions, the Seen or ego. Salvation occurs when the distinction between these two disappears and only the Seer remains. [76]

There is an overseer of the ego, watching and observing in a nonjudgmental manner. It is individualized spirit, the soul, the Seer. The ego will eventually tire of its role as protector and seek relief from its burden. When ego has finally exhausted itself and is willing to consider something else, a person will experience a state of release and the characteristics of the divine soul will fully emerge. It is our egos that are involved in driving most of our activities in life. It defines who we are within our social structure and culture. The relationship between our ego and our soul was illustrated to me during meditation one spring morning in 2011 in the following poem:

Enjoy your country

But don't be a national

Enjoy your religion

But don't be a convert

Enjoy your education

But don't be your profession

Be the Joy

You are the Joy

What is the Joy? I contend that it is spirit, divinity, creation flowing through us. The poem expresses the attitude we need to adopt to be happy in life. It tells us to focus on the Joy we feel. If you subscribe to the theory that all things are part of a perfect divine creation, infinite intelligence, then the ego must be part of that plan. However, recent studies of highly inflated egos, narcissism, conclude that it is a mental disorder that goes undiagnosed by our society. [77] Thus how can ego, referenced from ancient writings such as the Upanishads be part of such a divine plan? I would like to offer an explanation.

In nature, we see duality of expression everywhere. Magnetism flows between a separate north and south pole. Day follows night as night follows day. Without the night, we would not know the day. If there is no darkness, we cannot know and appreciate the light. The plant and animal kingdom express themselves through the duality of opposites, male and female.

Does this duality exist within our selves? Yes. Our countries, religions, and professions are what differentiate us, what make us different and separate from each other. This is the domain of our egos. The joy that comes from living these aspects of human existence well and to their fullest feels the same for everyone. This pleasure is our common thread. This is the domain of spirit. Have you ever seen a stadium full of jubilant hometown sports fans when their team wins the championship? They are celebrating a common feeling each one is experiencing at that moment. They are putting aside their separateness and egos. They are feeling joy and togetherness in that moment.

The ego generates attitudes of separateness and joy generates feeling of unity—this is our duality. The ego must develop so the individual soul can know its joy, its divinity. We need to know separateness before we can experience unity. Unity and separateness are opposites. When we start our early life immersed with the illusion of separateness, ego, we set ourselves up for the joyful realization and re-union with the fact that we are all created from the same spiritual divine source. Without darkness, we cannot know and appreciate the light.

Our egos develop so we can experience the true Joy of our souls.

Joy and Bliss

When Gopi Krishna described his Kundalini experience, he said he was in a "state of exaltation and happiness impossible to describe." Reading about other peoples' experiences with out-of-body sensations and mystical experiences, I have noticed they all refer to the difficulty in describing the feelings of the moment. Certainly my own experiences fall into this category. I can only describe them as spiritual orgasms!

After reading dozens of books and attending seminars about self-discovery through meditation, past life regression, and the study of universal laws, I still find myself asking a question. Not the one from my university days that was "Who are we?" I now know I am a spiritual being in a human body. The question today is "What is joy and bliss?" How do you describe that "state of exaltation?"

When I travel to English-speaking countries, I find the local accents charming, although at times a little difficult to understand. There are times when confusion seeps into the conversation. When I hear another visitor, a complete stranger, speaking with my accent, it is exciting and pleasing to hear. Someone from home!

Imagine, if you will, you are on holiday—yes again! This time you're in a very foreign land, isolated from the world and your language. You don't speak the local dialect. You are committed to staying several months because you paid all the expenses before leaving home, but you have absolutely no aptitude for foreign languages. After many weeks, you would no doubt feel a sense of separateness and loneliness. It is almost impossible to buy food that you like from the market because you do not speak the local language. Your ability to communicate with the locals is extremely limited. It is all hand gestures and body language. People are growing tired of your dance routines and are misinterpreting them. You experience a constant level of frustration. You begin to doubt your decision to come here. Why did I commit myself to this holiday? You wonder if you will last emotionally to the end of this journey. You regret ever being away from home.

Then one afternoon, feeling very despondent, tired, and alone, you're sitting in a café. The café where the waiter never brings you what you order! You suddenly hear at the next table your language. People speaking the language of your home! Words you understand! Words you have not heard for several months! What would you do?

I would guess, after the initial shock, that you would get up from your table and walk over to the strangers and introduce yourself. I suspect you would start to engage in a very animated conversation, delighted in the opportunity to speak your language for the first time in a very long time. Someone understands what you are saying! Someone is responding to you! It would be wonderful! How would you feel? I suspect you would feel very much alive, extremely happy and joyful, and perhaps be close to a "sense of exaltation impossible to describe."

This imaginary scenario of sudden unexpected familiarity is as near as I can come to describing the bliss I felt during my personal encounters with the Spirit of Creation when it touched the Soul of my Existence. Bliss appears as something we experience, something we are, a sense of Being in that moment, something that engulfs our emotional state. Bliss is the grown-up, adult version of Joy.

I often compare the spiritual journey to riding a bicycle. You can read all you want about riding, how to set the seat at the right height, the need for getting a little speed up before you start pedalling, learning balance, watching for potholes, and learning how the brakes work. But until you actually ride a bicycle and fall over, you cannot experience the thrill of riding. In his book, The Powers of Thought, Omraam Mikhael

Aivanhov references the value beyond just studying something. He states: "In order to live that vast, immense, rich life of the spirit you have to love it: it is not enough to understand it intellectually." [78] This concept is also reflected in the 14th verse of the book, Living the Wisdom of the Tao by Wayne Dyer. [79] When I read that passage, all that I had been reading over the years and what I had been trying to discover seemed to fall into place. The line is "You cannot know it, but you can be it."

This brought me back to the Sermon on the Mount in the New Testament where the beatitudes were presented. I thought perhaps a more appropriate spelling from the original translated version would be the be-attitudes.

Be the Joy!

Epilogue

Some days, I play a game. I call this game "I Saw God Today."

The game goes like this. I watch for people showing kindness, consideration, cooperation, thoughtfulness and selfless acts. For example, the other day I observed a young man picking up a package of paper towel that had fallen off a shopping cart that an elderly lady was pushing across the parking lot. He picked it up and ran towards her to give it back to her. She had not noticed it had fallen from the bottom of her cart. She was very thankful to the young man and gave him a big smile.

I was recently chatting with my neighbour when he noticed a very elderly neighbour out for his afternoon walk. The elderly man suddenly fell in the middle of the road. My neighbour stopped talking in mid-sentence and ran to see how the elderly gentleman was doing. He helped him back to his feet and accompanied him back to his home. Compassion and caring in action!

Yesterday, a young man with tattoos of colourful dragons on his arms and a silver earring through his eyebrow held the door to the mall open for me. I gave him a smile and said thank-you (for his consideration and kindness). My grey hair is finally paying off for something!

I look for people smiling in their day-to-day activities because when they smile they are acknowledging the Divine Presence within themselves and the people they are interacting with.

I smile at strangers, and most smile back. Some even beam back like the small child on his mother's hip in the grocery store. That was certainly an "I Saw God Today" moment.

Hearing someone laugh, watching a person make a donation to the food bank, or seeing other car drivers slow down to let someone else into the busy lane of traffic—these are all actions that express our sacred selves. We are experiencing that moment from the other person's perspective and responding in a kind and cooperative manner. A very simple decision, yet many choose to ignore that possible choice.

These types of activities show an understanding that we are all living a part of a greater existence. Showing kindness, consideration, and cooperation is Spirit in action. "I Saw God Today."

I see this creative force in other ways. I recently was waiting for my car to be serviced. I was in the waiting room reading a book. I glanced at another customer, also reading. I could see the rhythmic breathing of this person's upper body. This was divine energy, the creative force being expressed as respiration. I realized this energy is caring and intrinsic; it cannot be controlled. However, we as human beings can direct this energy through our thoughts and attitudes. If our thoughts and attitudes are clothed in kindness, tolerance, and promote the well being of others, we are expressing our Sacred Self. Our actions of generosity, practising patience and being helpful will also reflect this Spirit.

I often psychically pick up negative vibrations and energies from car drivers as they speed by me tailgating and cutting each other off. I can feel the anger of an argument in the local shopping mall when one person feels the other one spent too much money for an item or they are just having a general disagreement. This is not a pleasant experience. The emotions are very cold, unsettling, and disturbing, and they make me appreciate "I Saw God Today."

As long as we are alive as human beings, we do have to deal with ego energy, both within ourselves and from others. I often perceive ego energy as just a disguise for a lonely soul, someone who just wants to be appreciated. Recently, I was sitting in my doctor's office and a young man walked in. He approached two women who were sitting in the room, speaking very loudly. He started arguing with them. They appeared to be his mother and sister. He demanded they give him a cell phone because his had gone dead. Even though there are signs in the waiting room asking people not to use their cell phones, he spoke very loudly using language that others found offensive. He then proceeded to demand money from these women because all he had was foreign currency. He had badly scraped arms because he had been in a motorcycle race on the weekend and the foreign currency was part of his winnings. This very loud and obnoxious young man was causing great embarrassment to his family, and when he did leave the waiting room, you could almost hear the entire room whisper "Good riddance."

But I could sense in his eyes that all he really wanted was a little appreciation, a lost soul looking for attention and love. The sadness was he could not see the affection he was receiving from his family. They were responding to his requests with respect, patience, kindness, tolerance, and co-operation, not the qualities he was expressing that morning. He was expressing his ego, almost to the point of narcissism. He was irritating and annoying everyone in his vicinity. It was a very interesting dance to observe; the self-centered ego demands of the young man and the empathy and patience of his family that he could not perceive. These were foreign attitudes to him, not part of his consciousness. His totally selfish attitude was blocking his recognition of the love his family, albeit under some stress, was giving him.

When we step back from what appears to be our immediate stressful needs and remove ourselves from this daily task of survival for a few moments, we give ourselves a chance to see our indwelling Higher Conscious State. We can also learn to see this Energy in people around us, especially those who care for us.

My simple challenge to you, the reader, is to try this game "I Saw God Today." Choose a day and watch for smiles, displays of kindness, consideration, cooperation, thoughtfulness and tolerance. You will find it everywhere. You will get to know your Sacred Self. You will see that it is very real and an extremely pleasant aspect of our lives here on earth. I would like to leave you with a quote from the book Miracles Happen by Brian

Weiss and Amy Weiss:

> "This shift in perception from identifying with the body to identifying with the soul is a fundamental step on our journey. To know one's true nature is both freeing and healing. An ego or mundane mind can be easily afflicted by daily events and problems. But at the soul level, our deep calm is not affected by the minicatastrophes of everyday life or by other conflicts. A greater perspective allows peace to prevail and our hearts to remain open and loving." [80]

You can also participate in "I Saw God Today" by giving someone a smile, holding the door open for the person following behind you, letting someone into a busy lane of traffic, brushing the snow off the car windows of the car beside you in the parking lot, offering someone some encouragement, giving a sincere compliment to a stranger, visiting a shut-in center, or paying for the person's coffee who is standing next in line behind you. The opportunities are endless. Someone will probably smile at you.

Try playing "I Saw God Today." I know you will enjoy it.

Happy Living!

Conclusion

On December 13, 2012, during my morning meditation, the following came into my perception:

Imagine lying on a seaside beach, feeling the warmth of the sun on your body and the sand on your back. However, you are completely unaware of the vast ocean that lies just a few meters away. At first, the beach is very comfortable, warm, and very pleasing. As you lay there, you slowly get too hot, very thirsty, and extremely uncomfortable. But being unaware of the ocean, you just lay there getting irritated with the heat. You get very angry and start yelling at anything and everyone. Nothing changes. Eventually you reposition your body from lying on your back to sitting up, a small shift of perception of 90 degrees. You suddenly see the ocean and you recognize its cooling and soothing properties. Your discomfort disappears.

This is a metaphor for the relationship between matter (ego) and Spirit (soul, God). If we are not aware of the Spirit, symbolized as the ocean, we become uncomfortable and irritated. We do not necessarily know why and we don't really know what to do to relieve the discomfort. With no apparent solution in sight, our ego gets frustrated. We get grumpy and feel that "No one is looking after me properly." However, with just a small shift in our perception, we can see the ocean. We become aware of the presence of Universal Creative Intelligence, our Sacred Self. It is not something outside of us and available only through approved channels; it is part of our human nature and inner consciousness. It is totally accessible to all. The beauty is that the longer we are unaware of this Truth, the more grateful and heartfelt we are when we perceive this Divine Energy.

This seaside beach impression is not only a metaphor. It also shows us how to recognize our imprint of dependence on something physically greater than ourselves from infancy and childhood. As life's disappointments and discomforts accumulate in our psyches, if we don't make the shift in our understanding of the presence of Spirit in our lives, then we will continue to look for other people and organizations to relieve our discomforts, just as we did as infants and children. We need to take responsibility for our lives. When we expect others to provide for us, our approach is distorted and not focused properly.

In my mediation, I physically shifted my body. Nobody else on the beach came along and moved me so I would be able to see the ocean. It was an action initiated by myself. I addressed my discomfort—no one else did this for me.

We must make the effort. We are the ones who adjust our perceptions as we gain knowledge about life. No one can live our lives for us because that is our responsibility. When we approach the calming and cooling waters of the ocean, the Spirit, our demeanour changes and we become more at ease and at peace.

We exist on two planes simultaneously: the sphere of the body and its physical senses and the vastness of the Spirit, that higher consciousness that pervades everything. When we express thoughts and attitudes of self-responsibility, kindness, tolerance, compassion, respect and humility, we are expressing the divine spirit that resides within our bodies and consciousness. This is the source of our serenity, peace of mind, joy, and love.

Depth of awareness is an ongoing process. In this book, I have described my interactions with this Divine Energy. I hope you found the descriptions enlightening. I hope you have found a new expanded awareness within yourself. Everyday, I see a little bit more of our shared Intelligence. Everyday, I learn more about living with this Source. Everyday, I realize more and more that there is a Divine Intelligence available to us for guidance and protection as we journey through this life.

We are all created from the same spiritual material. What we do with this energy is as diverse as a field of colourful wildflowers on a high mountain meadow. The many colours, shapes, and contours of the meadow reflect back to us the diversity of human cultures and societies. We are not alone in this Universe or on this planet. We need only open our Inner Sight and be truly amazed!

Look and You Will See.

Celebrate those Moments in Time.

References

1. Dyer, Wayne *Wisdom of the Ages* New York: HarperCollins, 1998

2. Kieffer, Gene *Kundalini for the New Age* New York: Bantam, 1988

3. Burke, Maurice *Cosmic Consciousness* New York: Penguin, 1991

4. ACISTE. 21 Oct 2013. http://aciste.org/index.php/about-aciste/case-statement

5. Pew Forum "Many Americans Mix Multiple Faiths". 9 Dec 2009. 21 October 2013. http://www.pewforum.org/2009/12/09/many-americans-mix-multiple-faiths/

6. ACISTE. 21 Oct 2013. http://aciste.org/index.php/about-stes/what-is-an-ste

7. ACISTE. "Changes Following an STE". 21 Oct 2013. http://aciste.org/index.php/about-stes/changes-after-an-ste

8. ACISTE. "Common Challenges Following an STE". 21 Oct 2013. http://aciste.org/index.php/about-stes/common-challenges-of-an-ste

9. ARE. 21 Oct 2013. http://www.edgarcayce.org/are/edgarcayce.aspx

10. Galkowski, Victoria "Bone Stimulation for fracture healing: What's all the fuss". Indian J Orthop 2009 Apr-Jun. 21 Oct 2013. http://www.ncbi.nlm.nih.gov/pmc/articles/PMC2762251/

11. Weiss, Brian *Many Lives, Many Masters* New York: Simon & Schuster, 1988

12. Thurston, Mark & Fazel, Christopher *The Edgar Cayce Handbook* New York: Random House, 1992

13. The Forbidden Heights. 22 Oct 2013. http://www.forbiddenheights.com/main/catlayoutmythicguides/carl-gustav-jung

14. Doucleff, Michaeleen "Chopped: How Amputated Fingertips Sometimes Grow Back".12 Jun 2013. 22 Oct 2013. http://www.npr.org/blogs/health/2013/06/10/190385484/chopped-how-amputated-fingertips-sometimes-grow-back

15. Dossey, Larry *The Science of Premonitions* New York: Penguin, 2009

16. Dixon, Jana "Biology of Kundalini".2006. 22 Oct 2013. http://biologyofkundalini.com/article.php?story=Prana

17. Wikipedia. 22 Oct 2013. http://en.wikipedia.org/wiki/Synchronicity

18. Chopra, Deepak *The Spontaneous Fulfillment of Desire* New York: Random House, 2003

19. Fernandez, Manny "Surviving a Deadly Twister, Twice

in 65 Years." The New York Times. 16 Apr 2012. 24 Oct 2013. http://www.nytimes.com/2012/04/17/us/in-woodward-oklahoma-surviving-a-twister-twice-in-65-years.html?_r=0

20. Wikipedia. 9 Apr 2013. 24 Oct 2013. http://en.wikipedia.org/wiki/He_blew_with_His_winds,_and_they_were_scattered

21. Solitical. 24 Oct 2013. http://www.solitical.com/news/details/0cNf4NM22Z4za

22. 24 Oct 2013. http://machaut.uchicago.edu/?resource=Webster%27s&word=will&use1913=on

23. "How to build an Olympic champion: Be religious." BBC Sport. 25 Jul 2012. 24 Oct 2013. http://www.bbc.co.uk/sport/0/olympics/18893284

24. Chopra, Deepak *How to Know God* New York: Random House, 2000

25. ARE. 24 Oct 2013. http://www.edgarcayce.org/are/spiritualGrowth.aspx

26. Byrne, Rhonda *The Secret* New York: Simon & Schuster, 2006

27. Dooley, Mike *Manifesting Change* New York: Simon & Schuster, 2010

28. "All About Fear." Psychology Today. 27 October 2013. http://www.psychologytoday.com/basics/fear

29. Puff, Robert "Meditation for Modern Life." 27 Oct 2013. http://www.psychologytoday.com/blog/meditation-modern-life/201209/feeling-scared-try-mother-natures-fear-buster

30. Harpur, Tom *Water Into Wine* Toronto Canada: Thomas Allen, 2007

31. Goodreads. 27 October 2013. http://www.goodreads.com/quotes/309660-sometimes-things-fall-apart-so-that-better-things-can-fall

32. Chopra, Deepak *The Seven Spiritual Laws of Success* San-Rafael CA: Amber-Allen, 1994

33. Webster's Dictionary. 27 October 2013. http://machaut.uchicago.edu/websters

34. Open Bible. 27 October 2013. http://www.openbible.info/topics/marrying_a_divorced_person

35. Answers Corporation. 27 Oct 2013. http://wiki.answers.com/Q/When_did_Gandhi_say_Be_the_change_you_want_to_see_in_the_world

36. Pell, Arthur R. *Think and Grow Rich* Napoleon Hill New York: Penguin 2003

37. Fillmore, Charles "Teach Us To Pray." 27 Oct 2013. http://www.freehealingbooks.com/user/image/teach_us_to_pray_charles_fillmore.pdf

38. Braden, Gregg *The Divine Matrix* Carlsbad CA: Hay House, 2007

39. Merriam-Webster. 23 Oct 2013. http://www.merriam-webster.com/medical/altered%20state%20of%20consciousness

40. Wikipedia. 23 Oct 2013. http://en.wikipedia.org/wiki/Altered_state_of_consciousness

41. CBC News "Illegal drugs: Canada's growing

international market." 24 Jun 2009. 23 Oct 2013. http://www.cbc.ca/news/technology/illegal-drugs-canada-s-growing-international-market-1.798638

42. CDC "Policy Impact: Prescription Painkiller Overdoses." 19 Dec 2011. 23 Oct 2013. http://www.cdc.gov/homeandrecreationalsafety/rxbrief/

43. NHS "Statistics on Alcohol: England 2012." 31 May 2012. 23 Oct 2013. https://catalogue.ic.nhs.uk/publications/public-health/alcohol/alco-eng-2012/alco-eng-2012-rep.pdf

44. Gallup "Majority of U.S. Drink Alcohol." 17 Aug 2012. 23 Oct 2013. http://www.gallup.com/poll/156770/majority-drink-alcohol-averaging-four-drinks-week.aspx

45. NIH "Alcoholism." 13 Sept 2013. 24 Oct 2013. http://www.nlm.nih.gov/medlineplus/alcoholism.html

46. Bloomberg. 22 Mar 2013. 24 Oct 2013. http://www.bloomberg.com/news/2013-03-22/coffee-consumption-increases-in-u-s-association-survey-shows.html

47. Food Product Design ENERGY DRINKS SALES WILL SKYROCKET TO $21 BILLION BY 2017. 4 Feb 2013. 24 Oct 2013. http://www.foodproductdesign.com/news/2013/02/energy-drink-sales-will-skyrocket-to-21-billion-b.aspx

48. Gourmet Coffee Zone. 24 Oct 2013. http://gourmet-coffee-zone.com/coffee-facts.html

49. Wikipedia. 22 Oct 2013. 24 Oct 2013. http://en.wikipedia.org/wiki/Opium

50. Szalavitz, Maia "Hooked on Addiction." 15 Apr 2011. 24 Oct 2013. http://healthland.time.com/2011/04/15/hooked-on-addiction-from-food-to-drugs-to-internet-porn/

51. Wikipedia. 1 Nov 2013. 6 Nov 2013. http://en.wikipedia.org/wiki/Behavioral_addiction

52. 6 Nov 2013. http://www.sucht-news.at/en/nonsubstance_addiction

53. The Buddhist Center. 17 Dec 2013. https://thebuddhistcentre.com/text/what-meditation

54. NCCAM "Meditation: An Introduction." Jun 2010. 24 Oct 2013. http://nccam.nih.gov/health/meditation/overview.htm

55. NCCAM "Tai Chi: An Introduction." Jun 2010. 24 Oct 2013. http://nccam.nih.gov/health/taichi/introduction.htm

56. Wikipedia. 25 Oct 2013. 26 Oct 2013. http://en.wikipedia.org/wiki/Michelangelo

57. Wikipedia. 26 Oct 2012. 26 Oct 2013. http://en.wikipedia.org/wiki/List_of_popes

58. Allen, James *As A Man Thinketh* Avon MA: Adams Media, 2012

59. Wikipedia. 24 Oct 2013. 27 October 2013. http://en.wikipedia.org/wiki/Cuyahoga_River

60. Maag, Christopher "From the Ashes of '69, a River Reborn." The New York Times. 20 Jun 2009. 27 October 2013. http://www.nytimes.com/2009/06/21/us/21river.html?_r=0

61. Chopra, Deepak "5 Steps To Harness The Power Of Intention." 20 May 2013. 27 Oct 2013. http://www.mindbodygreen.com/0-9603/5-steps-to-harness-the-power-of-intention.html

62. Weiss, Brian *Many Lives, Many Masters* New York: Simon & Schuster, 1988

63. Myss, Caroline *Sacred Contracts* New York: Random House, 2002

64. Twain, Mark .22 Oct 2013. http://www.brainyquote.com/quotes/quotes/m/marktwain109919.html

65. Staff, Mayo Clinic "Forgiveness: Letting go of grudges and bitterness." 23 Nov 2011. 23 Oct 2013. http://www.mayoclinic.com/health/forgiveness/MH00131

66. Creagan, Edward T. "Forgiveness is the gift you give yourself." 22 Apr 2010. 23 Oct 2013. http://www.mayoclinic.com/health/forgiveness/MY01290

67. Barrowman, Jim "Stability of a Model Rocket in Flight." Centari Engineering 1970. 30 Oct 2013. http://www.rockets4schools.org/images/Rocket.Stability.Flight.pdf

68. McTaggart, Lynne *The Field* New York: HarperCollins, 2008

69. Wikipedia. 6 Aug 2013. 26 Oct 2013. http://en.wikipedia.org/wiki/Canadian_federal_election,_1984

70. Mitchell, David J. "Patronage Nation." *The Ottawa Citizen*. 27 June 2009. 26 Oct 2013. http://www.ppforum.ca/sites/default/files/OP-ED_Patronage_Jun_27.pdf

71. Thurston, Mark & Fazel, Christopher *The Edgar Cayce Handbook* New York: Random House, 1992

72. Weiss, Brian *Many Lives, Many Masters* New York: Simon & Schuster, 1988

73. Pulos, Lee & Richman, Gary *Miracles & Other Realities* San Francisco CA: Omega Press, 1990

74. Braden, Gregg *The Divine Matrix* Carlsbad CA : Hay House, 2007

75. 27 October 2013. http://www.ewtn.com/padrepio/mystic/bilocation.htm

76. V, Jayaram "The Soul, The Ego And The Process of Liberation." 27 October 2013. http://www.hinduwebsite.com/divinelife/essays/soulandego.asp

77. Pamoukaghlian, Veronica "Narcissism in High-Functioning Individuals-Big Ego or Severe Disorder?" 09 Nov 2010. 27 October 2013. http://brainblogger.com/2010/11/09/narcissism-in-high-functioning-individuals-big-ego-or-severe-disorder/

78. Aivanhov, Omraam Mikhael *The Powers of Thought* France: Dumas-Titoulet, 2006

79. Dyer, Wayne *Living the Wisdom of the Tao* Carlsbad CA: Hay House, 2008

80. Weiss, Brian & Weiss, Amy *Miracles Happen* New York: HarperCollins, 2012